The Mound People

1. Horned twin god
   from Grevensvænge

P. V. GLOB

The Mound People

Danish Bronze-Age Man Preserved

Translated from the Danish by
JOAN BULMAN

CORNELL UNIVERSITY PRESS
Ithaca, New York

© P. V. Glob, 1970.
This translation © Faber and Faber Limited, 1974.
First published 1974 by Cornell University Press.
Originally published in Denmark by Gyldendal, as *Højfolket:
Bronzealderens Mennesker bevaret i 3000 Ar.*

Library of Congress Cataloging in Publication Data
(For library cataloging purposes only)
Glob, Peter Vilhelm, date.
   The mound people.
   Translation of Højfolket.
   Bibliography: p.
   1. Bronze age—Denmark. 2. Denmark—Antiquities.
I. Title.
GN778.22.D4G5513   913.363   73-2602

ISBN 0-8014-0800-8

Printed in Great Britain

Med ham faldt Skovens skønneste Træ
For sidste Gang gav det den Døde Læ

Johannes V. Jensen

from
The Man in the Coffin:
The Bronze Age Grave
from Borum Eshøj

Fallen with him is the tree, the forest's pride,
The dead man's final shelter to provide.

Contents

Illustrations

13

ACKNOWLEDGMENTS

photographs
Danish National Museum *plates* 8, 12, 17, 18, 20, 21, 23, 24, 31 :
P. V. Glob *plates* 3, 4, 9, 26, 40, 42, 43, 47–49, 51–56, 58–63, 72–75 :
Hansen, Vamdrup *plates* 2, 33 : Lennart Larsen *plates* 37, 38, 57,
64–68, 71 : C. M. Lund *plate* 22 : Thomas Thomsen *plate* 19
drawings
J. Kornerup *plate* 7 : A. P. Madsen *plates* 5, 6, 10, 11, 13–16, 27–30,
32, 34–36, 41, 44, 50 : O. Sørling *plate* 39

15

1 · The Mound People Emerge

THE strange forces that preserved the Bog People for two millennia did the same for the Mound People for more than three. They were a Bronze Age people who ruled in Denmark before 1000 B.C. Whereas the Bog People of the Iron Age lay naked or only lightly clad in the bogs where they had been placed as sacrifices to the Great Goddess, the Mound People were buried in oak coffins in their everyday clothes, and were richly supplied with ornaments and weapons of gold and bronze under the splendid domes of the burial mounds that crown the highest hills throughout Denmark, dominating the landscape.

In both cases it was the bog water, deficient in oxygen but impregnated with tannic acid from the tree remains in the bogs—or from the heavy oak coffins themselves—that preserved the dead right up to the present day. While many of the Bog People are in a perfect state of preservation physically, stained a bronze colour by the bog water, and look as though they have only just fallen asleep, it is rarely possible to make out the facial features of the Mound People because nothing of them survives but the outermost, horny layer of the skin, the eyebrows and the hair. However, we are familiar with their faces from their small bronze sculptures.

The Bog and Mound People began to emerge from their hiding-places nearly two hundred years ago. One of the first of the Bog People was Queen Gunhild, who was discovered in Haraldskjær Fen in 1835. Her fame spread immediately

2. The oak coffin in Guldhøj

throughout the country; and she was given a coffin by King Frederick VI and taken to the church of St. Nicolaj in Vejle. Others had been found before her, accounts of Bog People having been known in Denmark since as early as 1773. The Mound People revealed their secrets more reluctantly. In many of the early oak coffins brought out there was no trace of a skeleton, only clothing, weapons and ornaments, so that it was believed the oak coffins were simply repositories for the dead person's possessions placed down in the middle of the great burial mounds to protect them against robbery, while the dead themselves were burnt and their ashes put into the urns which were in many instances found in the sides of the same burial mounds.

The first known oak coffin was discovered at Foldingbro Krogård in 1823, not far from the Konge river in southern Jutland, when a large burial mound was being razed to provide earth for road-making. In its side was found an urn containing burnt bones, and, in a pile of stones standing in water yellowed with rust, the bottom of an oak coffin nearly six and a half feet long—and empty. The discovery was at once reported to the Royal Commission for the Preservation of Antiquities but since there was nothing except earth in the coffin, no examination was undertaken on the spot.

The next oak coffin came to light in 1827 in Toppehøj, a burial mound close to the village of Bollerslev, south-west of Åbenrå. Treasure hunters had started investigating the mound, which is approximately sixteen feet high and ninety-eight feet wide, because a light had been seen burning there and it was thought that King Balder, from whom the village was supposed to have taken its name, was buried in it together with rich treasure. The grave-robbers had abandoned the attempt, but a farmer had then obtained the owner's permission to take earth from the mound. After he had removed a quarter of it, he had come upon a pile of stones covering an oak coffin, the lid of which he trod on and broke. That was where the treasure would be. As the coffin was full of water, he dug a channel to let it out and drove his spade through the

3. Stabelhøje on Mols, seen from the north-east

hole in the lid with the result that earth poured in and the objects inside emerged in complete disorder. That these were salvaged and that reliable information was obtained about the discovery was due to the parish priest of Bjolderup, J. H. Prehn, who immediately wrote a long report which included excellent drawings of the mound and the coffin and articles found in it. He also arranged for the objects to be sent to the 'Collection of Northern Antiquities' which was at that time housed in the loft of the Trinitatis church behind the Round Tower. The finds consisted of a cap and cloak of woven woollen material, a sword, dagger, axe and safety-pin of bronze, a comb made of a flat piece of horn, and a hollowed-out wooden vessel with two lugs. The discovery attracted a great deal of attention both on account of the many objects involved and because there was found with them a well-preserved lock of black human hair, though beyond that nothing—not the slightest trace of bones.

More oak coffins were found in south Jutland during the succeeding decades, but always as a result of the plundering or levelling of mounds, and never with an expert present. If rich finds were made, of the buried people themselves there were still few vestiges, and the mystery of the oak coffins remained unsolved. A coffin was discovered, for instance, on Stamplund Farm, west of Åbenrå, in 1837 that contained water, mud, clothes and hair. About ten feet long, it was left standing in the farmyard for a few years and then split and used as a loft above the cattle shed, where the pieces survived in such good condition that when the archaeologist Vilhelm Boye visited Stamplund in 1876, it was quite possible to visualize the coffin's original appearance. Some twenty years later a coffin surrounded by stones stained a reddish-brown was found in Nøragerhøj at Emmelev on the west coast. In this were a gold arm-ring, a bronze sword, woollen material, an animal hide and a cow's horn embedded in a wet, bluish-grey, clayey substance that 'gave off an offensive smell'. Samples of this were sent with the objects themselves to the Museum in Copenhagen. But in spite of a most careful examination no trace of human bones could be detected in it.

4. Stabelhøje on Mols, seen from Kalø

In the spring of 1860 Valdemar Thisted, the parish priest of Høirup (between Haderslev and Ribe), investigated an oak coffin in Lille Dragshøj at Vester Arnum, and was able for the first time to announce that a coffin had contained 'an unburnt body of a human being'. However, his encounter with one of the Mound People was not accepted by the experts on the grounds that not a single splinter of bone had been found in the coffin. It was unquestionably the large treasures of gold and silver said to have been found in burial mounds nearby that had tempted people to try digging in Lille Dragshøj, too. The first things they had come upon were pieces of heavy oak beams, but so much water had poured out of the mound that work had had to be abandoned. In the autumn of 1859, however, the owner of the property decided to use the earth in the mound to enrich the surrounding soil. After he had carted away about 1,500 waggon-loads of earth, or about a third of the mound, the men struck a large pile of stones and once more so much water gushed out that they had to stop work for a couple of hours. When they started again, the end of an oak coffin appeared. It was coated with a yellowish-brown substance. Almost at once it was hidden again by a fall of earth. News of the oak coffin reached Pastor Thisted who pursuaded the owner of the mound to leave it untouched until the following spring when he himself would be able to be present and take charge of operations. When spring came, the coffin was completely uncovered. Expectations of enormous riches were so great that the men hacked a hole in one end of the coffin smashing a wooden vessel ornamented with tin pins. Fortunately nothing further happened until Pastor Thisted arrived. The lid of the coffin was then raised with care so that its contents could be scrutinized. Inside lay the unburnt body of a human being that 'had sunk together into a glutinous, oily and in places fatty substance in which the forms could only be indistinctly discerned'. The pastor's account went on to say that 'the skull was still quite intact and the top of the head and the neck were covered with long, heavy coal-black hair'. The coffin was re-buried in the mound and not sent to Copenhagen

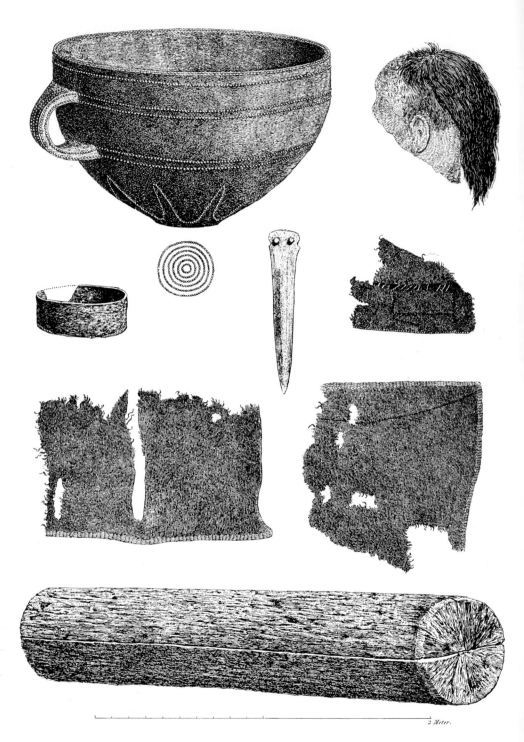

5. The oak coffin from Lille Dragshøj and its contents

until later on—when an examination showed that what was believed to be the skull was in fact the skin of a human head, although when it originally came to light this might have contained a well-preserved brain looking like a skull. Samples of the muscular tissue of the heart were also sent for examination. It was established that the dead man had been lying on an animal hide and had been wearing a cap, cloak and coat. On his chest lay a bronze dagger in a wooden sheath and beside his legs stood the wooden bowl which had been encountered first and had in it an oval bark-container. There was also a wooden double-headed fastener. No one realized that it was the great quantity of acid water that had totally eaten away the bones. All that remained of them was a 'peculiar, pale blue powder' that proved to consist of iron, together with phosphoric acid and a little sulphur.

When shortly afterwards, in an oak coffin in Fladshøj at Tobøl just north of the river Konge, all that was found was a single vertebra wrapped in animal hide, into which ten small bronze pins had been driven, people were tempted to wonder whether these oak coffins had been used solely for the interment of certain parts of the body. The following year, the Mound People were to reveal themselves without reservation.

In June 1861, King Frederick VII paid a visit to Jelling, where a commission of experts was carrying out an excavation of the great burial mounds of Gorm and Thyra. The king's interest in antiquities being well known, some men brought him a number of fine and unusually well-preserved objects found in an oak coffin in the large mound, Trindhøj, which stood beside the main Havdrup road, south-west of Kolding. Since they also told him that the coffin still stood in its place beside a smaller oak coffin as yet untouched, the king instructed the members of the commission to investigate the find more closely. These four—the archaeologists Worsaae and Herbst, the anatomist Ibsen and the artist Kornerup— went to Trindhøj in August of the same year to find the two oak coffins in place but sadly damaged. A square hole had been cut in the lid of the larger one so that a small boy could be lowered in to bring out the treasure it contained in the

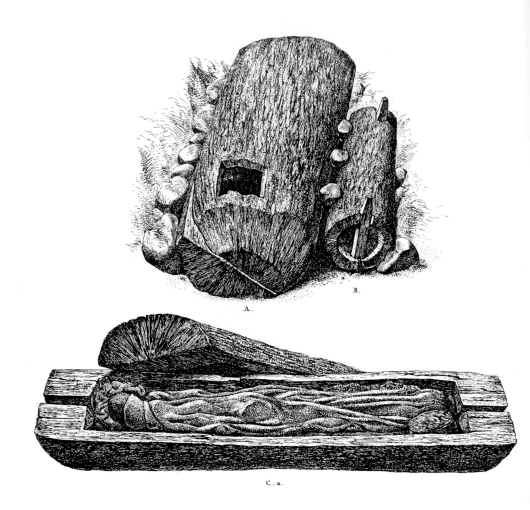

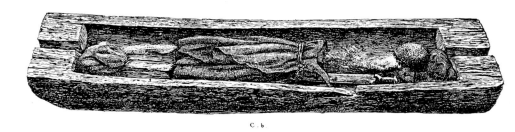

6. Oak coffins in Trindhøj

shortest possible time. The small coffin had been even more roughly treated. A chimney-scraping implement had been used to rake out the contents through one end, and so all that remained when the archaeologists lifted the lid was a small bronze bracelet. None the less, it was very important that both coffins could be measured and examined in their original positions in the mound, as may be seen from Kornerup's drawing done on a rainy day—17th August. This shows the *nisse* (pixy) of the mound cocking a snook at the archaeologists toiling eagerly away, because he knew of course that the coffin was empty but that concealed in the mound behind his back was yet another coffin, which was untouched. The further excavation of the considerable remaining part of Trindhøj was entrusted to a neighbouring farmer, who at the beginning of October of the same year was able to inform the commission at Jelling that he had found a coffin containing woollen material. Only a bark-container had been removed before the lid had been put back on the coffin and the whole covered over with wooden planks, tarpaulins and straw. Worsaae, Herbst and Kornerup at once left Jelling for Trindhøj, where the first scientific investigation of an oak coffin took place. In it lay a man in perfectly preserved costume, wrapped in a cow-hide. His bones, of which only a few fragments remained, were reduced to a pale blue powder, and the fleshy parts to a 'brown, soft, fatty mass'. Inside his cap lay the hair of his head and the whole of the brain, which was so well preserved that all its convolutions could be seen. In addition to the clothing, the coffin had in it a bronze sword in a wooden scabbard lying by the man's left side, and by his right foot a large basket containing a smaller basket, a cap, a bronze razor and a horn comb with twenty-four teeth. The oak coffin and its contents may be seen in the National Museum in the large Bronze Age gallery, where the Mound People reign supreme. Since Trindhøj had been excavated at the order of King Frederick VII and at his personal expense, all the finds were sent to the king, who had already been presented with the first objects found there, including a fine bronze sword, a large fibula and

Commissionen fra Illinge lader udgrave to Egekister i en Høi ved Vamdrup, den 15 August 1861.   J Kornerup fecit, 17 Aug 1861.

7. The excavation of Trindhøj

a double-headed fastener of bronze inlaid with amber with spiral ornamentation. The following year the king handed everything over to the Museum of Northern Antiquities, accepting in exchange two Bronze Age gold vessels and a few other items.

The Danish newspaper *Berlingske Tidende* reported the find on 29th October 1861: 'As mention has already been made of the excavation of Treenhøi on Hafdrup Farm in the parish of Vamdrup, it will doubtless interest our readers to learn that the continuation of the excavation of this mound was entrusted by His Majesty the King to Farmer Thomsen of Hjarup Farm. The mound has now been completely excavated to an area of thirty-two square feet and a depth of ten feet and a further coffin of about ten feet long was found. In this coffin was the entire skeleton of a man, fully clothed, with a bronze sword at his side. The bones had disintegrated, but

28

the clothing was so well preserved that, together with the coffin, it could be sent to Copenhagen where it will be kept in His Majesty's private collection of antiquities. This find has great scientific importance since it is the first that has provided actual proof that during this period, about two to three thousand years ago, bodies were buried in the coffins.'

During the excavation of Trindhøj, it was revealed that thirty years previously an oak coffin had been discovered in the south-westerly edge of the mound in such good condition that it had been used on the farm for a number of years as a watering trough. Altogether, four coffins were found in this mound, which must therefore have been a family burial place for the Mound People. The first coffin found probably contained the wife, for there is a letter in the archives of the National Museum stating that it contained, 'apart from a few trifles, a small pair of bronze tweezers'. The two large coffins housed two of the Mound People's chieftains, one of them with his daughter by his side in a small oak coffin.

2 · The Family in Borum Eshøj

BORUM ESHØJ lies on a range of hills with sweeping views in every direction about nine or ten miles north-west of Århus, and was once one of the largest Bronze Age mounds in Denmark, though little of it now remains. From its base, three oak coffins have been recovered at various times, containing specially well-preserved Mound People—an old man and an elderly woman, possibly a married couple, and a younger man who may have been their son.

In 1850, when the owner was removing earth from the eastern side of Borum Eshøj, then about twenty-nine and a half feet high and about 125 feet across, he came upon a stone coffin that had in it a bronze sword and various other bronze objects, whereupon he halted work. A couple of years later, in spite of the owner's protests, the Highway Authority removed some stones from the foot of the mound claiming it was entitled to do so under the provisions of a regulation of 1793. When it threatened to continue the work of destruction through the summer of 1853, the owner went to Copenhagen where he was given an audience with King Frederick VII. He presented him with the bronze sword from the stone coffin and was granted a protection order for the mound. A few years afterwards, Højballe Farm, on whose land Borum Eshøj lies, was sold and as the authorities had neglected to include the preservation order among the deeds, the new owner before long started digging in the mound. He too was to find a stone coffin, in the bottom of which lay a heap of

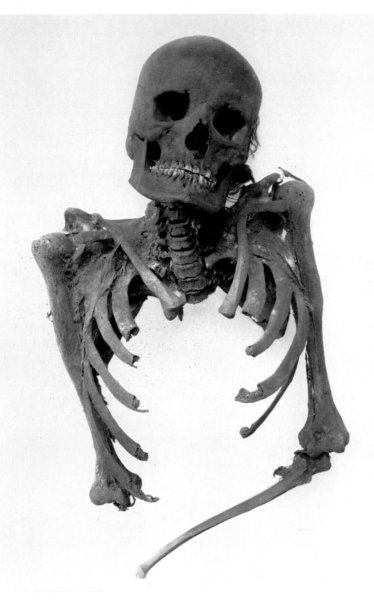

8. The old man from Borum Eshøj

9. All that remains of Borum Eshøj

burnt human bones and various articles of bronze: a dagger and a long pin, and two knives—one with a gold band twisted round the handle.

The rich soil of the mound later tempted yet another owner to cart it off to spread on his land, and that was how an oak coffin came to be revealed in the spring of 1871. For a long time it was left untouched as it was thought to be merely the trunk of an oak tree. It was so strong that it had remained intact even when the heavily-laden farm carts had been

C
33

10. The Borum Eshøj woman's costume

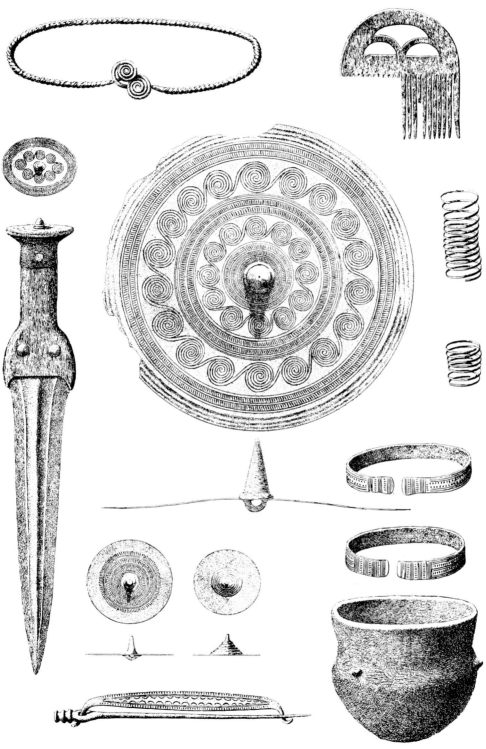

11. Her equipment

driven over it. After a time, however, the trunk got in the way of the carts. When the men tried to move it they discovered that it was a coffin with a lid and they flung themselves on it to grab the treasure they expected to find inside. After first raking it through with forks and fire-tongs they turned it upside down so that all its contents fell out, and bones and pieces of clothing were scattered far and wide. A skull was removed, to be discovered later in a loft in the village of Lading, while the hair and a few teeth were found in Skjoldelev. The owner himself took charge of a few well-preserved bronze objects in the belief that they were gold. Subsequently, when he tried to sell them to a goldsmith in Århus, he learnt that they were bronze and was referred to the Committee of the Friends of the Society for Historical and Antiquarian Collections (Selskabet for den historisk-antikvariske Samling), three members of which immediately set out for Borum Eshøj. They took possession of the coffin and everything that had been inside it, and gathered all the information they could about the discovery. In spite of the brutal treatment it had had, it was possible practically to reassemble the contents of the coffin, which were among the best ever found. The find consisted of the skeleton of an elderly woman wearing a dress of woollen material and richly provided with bronze objects. When one looks at these remains in the National Museum today, it is hard to understand how the textiles and bronzes, which are more than three thousand years old, can be in such good condition after the treatment they received.

As this oak coffin was found on the eastern side of Borum Eshøj, it was assumed that there must be more like it in the mound. The preservation order, which had never been respected, was accordingly lifted and in the summer of 1875 the archaeologist Conrad Engelhardt began to excavate the central area. He succeeded in finding two more well-preserved oak coffins.

At the centre, in the natural yellow clay, stood the oak coffin over which the mound had originally been raised. The trunk, which was nine feet long and had been split length-

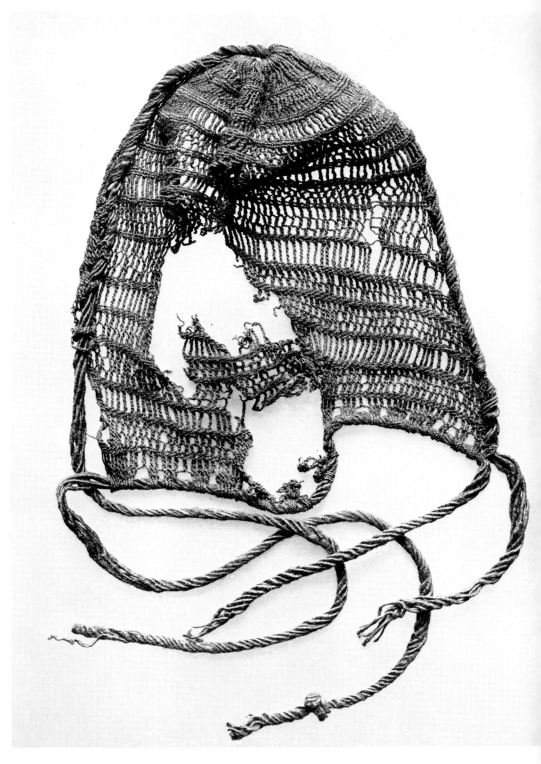

12. The Borum Eshøj woman's hair-net

ways so that one half formed the base of the coffin and the other the lid, had been carefully stripped of its bark, the chips lying round about indicating that this had been done on the spot. Further evidence for this seems to be provided by a hazel stick 30·9 inches long which was found close to the northern side of the coffin and which had notches cut along its side. Measuring from one end, the first and second notches were at intervals of six inches, the third notch being twelve inches from the second and six from the far end. There can be little doubt that it was a Bronze Age measuring rod marked out in feet, which was used in the construction of the coffin and possibly also in the laying out and erection of the mound.

From a telegram sent to the director of the Museum of Northern Antiquities, it is clear that the coffin was not opened until the necessary experts were present:

'CHAMBERLAIN WORSAAE
HAGESTED FARM NEAR HOLBÆK
BY MESSENGER ON HORSEBACK
BORUM 14TH SEPTEMBER 1875
OAK COFFIN FOUND. OPENING FRIDAY 12 O'CLOCK S.V.P.*
HAVE INFORMED PETERSEN AND STEFFENSEN

ENGELHARDT.'

Petersen was the museum's draughtsman and Steffensen the conservator.

Inside the coffin lay a man with his head to the west, his legs extended to the east and his arms at his sides, as is shown in the drawings done by Magnus Petersen as soon as it was opened. On his head he wore a round-crowned, woollen cap with inserted pile; his very dark hair had once been blond but had been stained by the tannic acid, which had also coloured the bones. The nose had been large and prominent, but there was no trace of a beard and he must have been clean shaven. The teeth, though worn, showed no signs of decay, and the nails had been well kept. The muscles

* S'il vous plait.

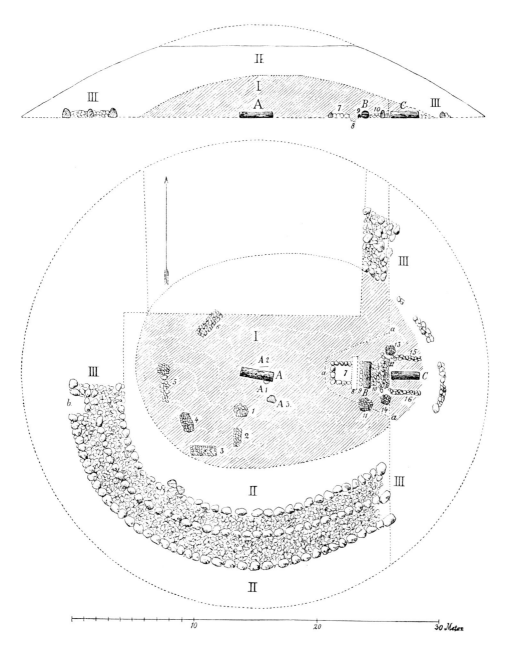

13. Ground plan of Borum Eshøj

and other fleshy parts still held the bones firmly together. In his memoirs, Magnus Petersen describes the problems of preservation:

'The coffins were lifted carefully, the bodies taken out and packed separately with great care in wooden packing cases which we had obtained from the village shop. But we found ourselves in some difficulty over the skeleton of the older man, for whereas the bones of the young man's skeleton fell apart when lifted up, the older man's bones were tightly embedded in the dried muscles which held them like thongs. The shop-keeper's wooden packing cases were not large enough to hold a fully extended body, so that I was obliged—at Engelhardt's request, as he himself was a little nervous of touching this body —to cut through the man's muscles with a knife between the lowest lumbar vertebra and the *os sacrum*, thus dividing the body into two halves to get it into the packing cases. I managed this quite successfully because it was not of course the first time I had dealt with dead bodies.'

Examination showed the man to have been between fifty and sixty years of age and five feet seven and a half inches tall, and to have had some difficulty in walking owing to rheumatism.

He lay on cow-hide which must have been freshly flayed as it was covered with maggot skins. Presumably the cow had been eaten at a 'funeral feast' before the building of the mound. Apart from the cap, he wore only a woollen loincloth held with a girdle tied in a loop. A round-cut woollen cape had been laid over him and at his feet were two pieces of woollen material with braided edges. The only other object was a wooden pin two and a half inches long, stuck into the side of the cape.

In August of the same year a well-preserved oak coffin, seven feet eleven inches long, was found between the old man's oak coffin and the woman's grave, though closer to the latter, which had been the initial find. This too had had its bark stripped off, but it was laid north to south and had been placed there later than the old man's coffin. Round it were various deposits of stones and among them

14. The young man from Borum Eshøj

chips of wood and an oak stump, which perhaps indicates that it, too, was finished on the spot. Engelhardt wrote to Worsaae about the discovery on 2nd August 1875: 'An oak coffin has just been found in Borum Eshøj. It was packed round with stones. Both ends have now been freed and water poured out of them.' The coffin was opened on 7th August, and another letter sent to Worsaae: 'At two o'clock yesterday afternoon the coffin was opened in the presence of a large gathering. The best preserved skeleton I have yet seen lay there dressed in a shirt which was held together by a (corroded) leather belt with a well-preserved wooden button. In his left arm, which was bent, lay a beautifully ornamented wooden scabbard, but our expectations of finding a bronze sword were dashed for, strangely enough, there was only a bronze dagger, whose handle had disintegrated. The right arm lay outstretched beside the body. The remains of a wide leather baldric lay over the right shoulder. Below the left shoulder was a well-preserved bone comb with the upper part pierced. By the right side of the head, and a little above it, there was a lidded bark-container, also in good condition. The whole was covered with a voluminous woollen shroud and over this an animal's (an ox's?) hide with the sides tucked under the body. At the feet were traces of sandals . . .' A wooden pin was found, as had been the case with the old man's cape.

He was evidently a young man since none of the teeth were decayed and the wisdom teeth were cutting through. He was about five feet six inches tall and on the skull his hair, skin and eyebrows were preserved. The bronze dagger, which was only six and a quarter inches long, lay in a scabbard measuring two feet four inches and was remarkable for being decorated with grooves along the face. It seems reasonable to assume that the young man's own sword had been handed down to a kinsman, having perhaps originally belonged to the older man, who might have been his father, and who lay weaponless in his coffin.

The old woman's coffin, which had received such rough treatment when it was found in 1871, lay on the eastern side of Borum Eshøj barely thirty-two and a half feet from the edge of the mound. That its rich contents were saved, apart from a few items, was due to their exceptional state of preservation and not least to the men from Århus who set out without delay and rescued what still remained of it, and parts of the skeleton and pieces of clothing. They also secured information about the circumstances of the find, which was immediately written down. The twenty-page report, with three plates of drawings, 'The Borum Find of April 1871: Report by cand. phil. A. Simesen', is still in existence. It is very detailed and contains important information which it was only possible to record because it was gathered at once and on the spot. It states that 'according to legend, a Prince Buris lies buried in the mound, from whom the village of Borum took its name . . . The actual mound is one hundred and eleven metres in circumference and about nine metres high. Around the foot was a circle of enormous stones which have now vanished, though traces of them still remain'. A note is added: 'In all the measurements I have used the French metric system. One metre equals about thirty-eight Danish inches'. This shows that Simesen was ahead of his time, for the metric system was only introduced into Denmark by law on 4th May 1907. His metric measurements were also converted in the margin into *alen* (two feet) and feet and inches when his information was entered in the museum archives.

The old woman's coffin lay in an east-west direction about five feet beneath the surface of the mound and in 'a bluish-black fatty earth mass, the rich soil referred to above'. It was eight feet long with the lower part finished diagonally at the ends. The first thing to be seen when the lid was removed was a 'burial urn of burnt clay' which stood roughly in the middle of the coffin and contained 'a black, muddy liquid mixed with earth that appeared to contain more solid components'. Uppermost in the coffin was an animal hide (probably cow) with the hairs still intact, which had 'grooves made in it, as though it had been scraped with some tool or other; or they may possibly have been the impress of the

43

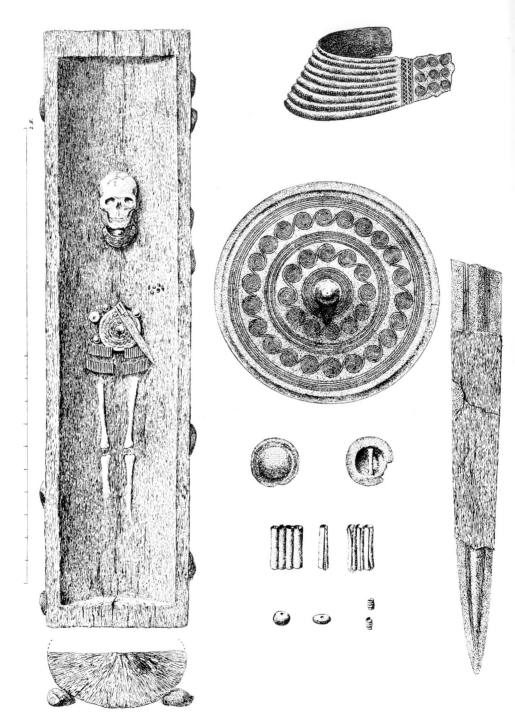

15. The woman from Ølby

vertical ridges in the oak bark'. Underneath was a large woollen rug in plain open weave, heavily fulled but not shaped or made up. The skeleton of the dead woman lay beneath this, dark-coloured and in good condition, in the brown woollen clothing she had been wearing. On the upper part of her body she wore a short tunic with elbow-length sleeves, and below, an ample, full-length skirt joined in front by a very clumsy seam stitched with five strands of woollen yarn. Round her waist was tied a belt eight feet two inches long, finished at both ends with an elaborate tassel. There was also another belt, in addition to various fragments of clothing difficult to identify, whose position in the coffin could not be definitely ascertained. The same also applied to remains of a large-mesh net of woollen thread. Beside the skull lay an abundance of hair up to two and a half feet in length and enclosed in a peculiar hair-net made by what is known as 'sprung' technique (*sprang*). A comb cut from a piece of horn which originally had twenty-one teeth is said to have been found beside the hair.

A number of well-preserved bronze objects were found in the coffin as well: a fibula ornamented on the top, a dagger with a horn handle nearly ten inches long, a belt disc (*tutulus*) decorated with a spiral pattern and a raised spike, a twisted neck ring with a spiral clasp, two arm rings made of flat, ornamented bronze bands, two spiral finger rings and two small bronze discs with raised spikes. In addition there is said to have been a wooden box in the coffin, which has since been lost, although all the other objects are still extant. All that is known of their position in the coffin is that the fibula was used to fasten the front opening of the tunic, and that the belt disc, from the evidence of a circular impression, lay over the waist front of the long skirt. How the other ornaments were worn is indicated by other oak coffin finds, among them a find from a mound at Ølby, north-west of Køge, one of the few from the Islands, in which parts of the oak coffin and the skeleton have survived. Round the neck was a bronze collar and on the stomach a belt disc surrounded by four small bronze ornaments similar to those found in Borum Eshøj;

2.   1.

16. The old man from Borum Eshøj

17. His costume

above that, instead of a dagger, the point of a sword blade in a wooden scabbard. Beneath the belt disc lay two rows of bronze tubes, about a hundred and twenty-five of them in all, which may have adorned the lower edge of a corded skirt like the one worn by the Egtved girl.

The richly provided woman in Borum Eshøj was aged between fifty and sixty and was about five feet two inches tall. Her hair was fair and long, fairer than the men's, and the bones show her to have been well built.

The unusually good state of preservation of all three oak coffins in Borum Eshøj and of the people buried in them is due to the fact that they rested in a smaller mound of water-repellent material, so that a layer of hard-pan quickly formed both above and below. This not only kept out the oxygen but largely protected them from water seeping down, for it was water that completely washed away the calcium of the bones in most of the other oak coffins. A ring of large stones was set around this inner mound, and then the large mound of earth was thrown up on top, making one of the largest Bronze Age mounds known in Denmark.

The Borum Eshøj of today is only a small remnant of the great domed burial mound that once covered the three oak coffins, but from its top there is still the same sweeping view over wide areas of Jutland that there was in the days of the Mound People. To the east and south-east one can look across now, as one could then, to their kinsfolk who lie buried under Stabelhøje on Mols on the other side of Århus Bay, and under Jelshøj, which crowns the range of hills south of Århus. The open country to the west, where fields and woods alternate in a rich mosaic right away to the high horizon around Himmelbjerg, closely resembles the Bronze Age parkland. For the past few centuries the range of hills on which Borum Eshøj lies has been under the plough, but all around, among the pastures, the cornfields and the straight rows of beet, areas of raised ground mark the sites of about ten of the Mound People's burial places, some of which were once as large as Eshøj, although they were levelled long ago.

High up in the blue above the top of Borum Eshøj the lark trills the song the Mound People heard three thousand years ago, while in summer many different-coloured wild flowers cover the sides of the mound—last refuge of the Bronze Age flora from the plough.

3 · The Women from Egtved and Skrydstrup

Two discoveries in particular bring us face to face with the women of the Mound People and make the three thousand years which separate us insignificant. These are the oak coffin finds from Egtved and Skrydstrup in south Jutland. They are unique. Nothing like them is known anywhere else in the world. The two finds provide an astonishing picture of the high-born ladies of a distant age—a picture preserved through so many centuries because whenever destruction threatened it was always unexpectedly averted. One is almost tempted to believe that the powers that ruled over the fortunes of the Mound People kept their potency for a very long time.

On 24th February 1921, Peter Platz, the owner of Egtved Farm, addressed a letter to the 'Old Northern Museum, Copenhagen', to the following effect: 'While moving a very large old burial mound on my land today, I came upon a hollowed-out tree-trunk with a lid which I presume to be an ancient burial. In case this is of any interest to the museum, I have stopped work on the excavation until I hear from you, which I hope will be soon.' It was then thirty years since the last well-preserved oak coffins had come to light—the three oak coffins which Vilhelm Boye, the brother-in-law of the writer Holger Drachmann, had excavated in 1891 in the large mound known as Trindhøj, north of Vamdrup Mill on the Konge river. Dr Sophus Müller, the famous and dreaded director of the National Museum since 1892, who was about to retire, immediately passed the letter on to his

18. The Egtved girl

19. Layer of hard-pan in a section through the Egtved mound

colleagues with the note: 'K.K. [Dear Colleagues], (*Quickly* hand to hand). Someone must go at once. Who wants to? and: When? S.M.' Of course the old campaigner expected the letter to act as a starting-gun in the race to Egtved, but here he was wrong. The letter went first to his right-hand man and successor as Keeper of the Department of Antiquities, who replied: 'Suggest matter postponed until May, area excavated to be filled in again; possibly small compensation for leaving mound untouched till then. Agreement in writing to be obtained from owner.' This was 'seconded' by the signatures of his colleagues and a letter was sent to Peter Platz, who replied by return: 'Have received your communication of the 25th instant. The coffin has been covered over again as requested, but if it is possible for you to come at once I should be most grateful as most of my men are engaged in carting the mound away, which means that most of it has already gone—so the coffin is very nearly exposed. Hoping to hear from you again.'

As soon as Sophus Müller read this letter he sent it on with the message: 'Colleagues! re the enclosed letter I must unfortunately request one of you to go over immediately (have asked Rosenberg without success). Who most wants to go?' Even this exhortation met with a chilly reception from most of his colleagues—'unfortunately'—'unable'—'willing to go but am unwell'; all but the Museum's senior inspector, Thomas Thomsen, who wrote: 'Have nothing against going, but will not stand in the way if others are more eager.' He was working then on the ethnographical collection, of which he was in charge, but was constantly taking part in excavations all over the country.

Before long, Thomas Thomsen was on his way to wintry Jutland and to the find that was to immortalize his name in Danish archaeology. On the morning of Saturday 5th March, the coffin was raised, photographed and brought under cover before snow fell that night.

It must have been a magnificent sight when the oak coffin, a good six and a half feet long, slightly curved and stripped of its bark, stood revealed on its bed of stones, as recorded in Thomas Thomsen's excellent photographs. The wood enclosed its contents tightly, for the log had been split in the direction of the grain and neither half had been smoothed off. A single uneven line running round all four sides was the only indication that it had been split. The outstanding condition of the coffin was due to the fact that it had stood in a smaller mound of meadow soil in which a layer of hard-pan had formed that had totally sealed it against the effects of oxygen, like the contents of a tin of preserves. But this protective layer of iron had been broken through when the work of levelling the mound started, so that within a few years it would have completely disintegrated. It was fortunate, therefore, that the coffin had been reached so swiftly. It was so strong that only a few of the lid's wood fibres had perished—without actually forming a hole—even though before anyone had any idea of its existence horses and carts had been driven over it during the removal of the earth. It had had a covering of a mere six to eight inches. Before excavation, only the western end of the coffin was exposed, from which poured out quantities of water containing the humic acid that had preserved the contents of wood and horn.

After the coffin had been measured and photographed on its bed of stones, the lid was raised with care to make sure that none of the contents would come to harm during its transportation to the laboratories of the National Museum in Copenhagen. In spite of the fact that he was ill at the time, Peter Platz got up in order to be present at the opening of the coffin, and he was one of the first to see its contents. The lid had fitted so tightly that not a speck of earth had worked its way inside. Everything was exactly as it had been when it was closed over the dead body three thousand years earlier.

Uppermost was a covering of animal hair which extended over the whole of the inside of the coffin. At the ends and in patches elsewhere, glimpses of woven material could be seen under this. Of the body itself nothing was visible, though if the woollen material at the western end of the coffin was lifted a little, the hair of the head could be seen. A cylindrical, lugged birch-bark bucket—obviously the last thing to have been placed inside for the use of the dead person before the coffin was closed—stood on top of the skin in one corner. A thin coating of a light substance that looked like white paint covered the inside of the coffin and showed in crevices on the outside. Chemical analysis revealed that this was a fatty substance from the body, deposited by the water that had filled the coffin.

Only the birch-bark bucket was removed, after which everything was carefully covered over with sheets of white tissue-paper, with a packing of straw on top, before the lid was replaced. The following day, a Sunday, was devoted to building a wooden case round the coffin, and packing it about with straw so that it stood immovable inside. On the Monday, the owner's sons and all those who had taken part in the excavation drove the coffin to Limskov railway station on the Grindsted-Vandel-Vejle line which would take it direct to Copenhagen.

It was naturally disappointing for Peter Platz that he was unable to be present at the final investigation of the coffin, but he fully understood that this could not be done except at the National Museum where the best facilities were available. It was due to him that the museum acquired for the first time an undisturbed oak coffin for laboratory examination. For this reason his name will always be linked with the Egtved find.

As soon as the coffin was safely housed in the National Museum, the elaborate investigation began under the leadership of Thomas Thomsen, assisted by two able conservators, Gustav Rosenberg and Julius Raklev. When it was reopened, it was quickly apparent that all that remained of the cow-hide which had covered the dead body was the layer of hair and the outermost, horny membrane of the skin. The skin itself had been eaten right away by the acid water that had filled the coffin. Fortunately, the cow-hide had been folded together with the skin side outermost, so that this could be replaced by a gelatine solution which bound the covering hairs together, enabling the hide to be rolled aside and the contents of the coffin to be revealed. Beneath it lay a

20. The Egtved coffin undisturbed, and with the rug removed

large piece of woollen material, folded together lengthwise and covering the whole of the coffin. The lumpy surface of this rug indicated what lay underneath. There was a bulge at each end showing where the head and feet would be, and a small bulge in the middle at the spot where a bronze belt disc decorated with a spiral pattern was later found to be lying. By the head, the edge of a small bark container could be seen, and to one side, at the foot, was a slightly raised area which proved to conceal a remarkable bundle of material. The large rug was made of brown sheep's wool, measuring eight feet in length and five feet five inches and six feet three inches in width at the ends, in plain weave, and hemmed along all the edges. Fragile as it was after lying there for three thousand years, it was possible to roll it up from the head over a piece of waxcloth.

Gradually, as the rug was rolled away, the body itself came into view. First the shoulder-length, loose-hanging hair of a girl became visible. Although now a brownish colour, stained by the acid water, it had originally been fair. The hair hid her face, but when it was lifted aside, her fine profile, held by the facial skin, was still preserved as well as her strong, well-shaped teeth, while the curve of her neck was marked out by the lines of the tendons. All this can be seen in the photographs. Underneath the hair, the brain was intact and behind the neck was a cord nearly fifty-one inches long made from three twisted strands of fine black sheep's wool—possibly her hair-band. The girl's head rested on the right cheek, and by her left ear lay a comparatively small bronze earring, the only one of its kind in the coffin. Examination of the teeth showed that she was aged between eighteen and twenty when she died.

By the girl's face stood a small oval container of lime-tree bark, sewn together with lime-tree bast. It held a bronze awl with a wooden handle, a net with lozenge-shaped meshes made from brown sheep's-wool thread knotted onto horse-hair taken from the tail or mane, a few burnt human bones, a little heather, moss, and a leaf which could not be precisely identified. The awl may possibly have been a toilet article, or

58

it may have been used to bore holes in bark containers, while the net was a hair-net.

As the rug was rolled down, the upper part of the girl's body could be seen dressed in a tunic with short sleeves and a straight, unbroken neck-line, woven in brown sheep's wool. She was evidently lying on her back with her arms at her sides. There were bronze rings round her wrists, a heavy, open ring without ornamentation on the left one, and, round the right, a flat arm ring with a hook clasp and decorated with five parallel rows of beads. Between the arm rings lay a belt disc patterned with spirals and with the raised spike pointing upwards. She had apparently been wearing this around her stomach. Underneath it could be seen her horn comb with its fretted design on the semi-circular upper part and its twenty strong teeth. Round her waist was knotted a woven belt exactly six and a half feet long and about three quarters of an inch wide, with an intricate tassel at one end. Her waist measurement was just over twenty-three and a half inches, so that she was both young and slender. Her nails were carefully rounded and well cared for, and she was five feet three inches tall.

Underneath the lowest part of the belt disc and wound twice round her body was a knee-length corded skirt made, like all the other articles of clothing, of brown sheep's wool. This extraordinary garment was only fifteen or sixteen inches long. The strands were gathered together at the top and bottom in an elaborate edging, and the top of the skirt was tied in front with a knotted bow, but otherwise hung loose. On the right-hand side it still followed the gentle curve of the hip. As all the hair was preserved, there were small tufts in the arm-pits, and in the groin—an inch and a quarter below the upper edge of the corded skirt—a patch three inches wide by three and a half inches long running down to a point. The outline of the legs was marked by the skin, and it could be seen that the skirt had sagged between them, while the cow-hide on which the girl lay formed a fold above.

The shape of the feet, the right one turned slightly inwards, could also be discerned. They were merely wrapped in pieces of irregularly shaped cloth without any sort of stitching but twisted and shaped into a certain resemblance of proper footwear, two pieces to each foot.

When the cow-hide was lifted aside, the bulge that had been noticed earlier under the covering rug proved to be a bundle containing the burnt bones of a child eight or nine years old, or possibly a little older. This may be also where the pieces of bone came from that were found in the bark container which had been placed by the girl's face. As the difference in age between the two cannot have been more than about ten years, the child could not have been the girl's but was probably a young serving-girl who was placed at the foot of the coffin beside the girl's left shin. She must thus be regarded as a sacrifice in her honour, such as is known from contemporary graves in Norway and Sweden. As to whether the little girl followed her mistress to death of her own free will or not, we can only guess.

At the bottom of the small cylindrical basket of birch-bark which had been placed last in the coffin, and which stood at the foot on top of the cow-hide, was a thick brown deposit. On analysis, this proved to be the dried remains of a drink, a mixture of beer and fruit wine, which had been brewed from wheat and cranberries or mountain cranberries, spiced with bog myrtle, and with honey added—the honey appeared in the deposit in the form of a quantity of pollen of, amongst others, lime-tree flowers. The sugar content of the honey would have made the drink alcoholic, while the bog myrtle would have acted as a preservative and given it flavour. It was a strong festive drink that was the final thing to be deposited in the young woman's coffin.

The Egtved girl was barely twenty when she lived her last summer in the fair river valleys of Egtved and Vejle, where so many of her kinsmen came to rest under the domed burial mounds along the hilly ranges to the east. Her coffin lay under Storhøj, which in its time was about thirteen feet high and ninety-nine feet in diameter, and which lies in the southern part of that large area which the Mound People inhabited. It originally consisted of more than fifty huge mounds, most of them now levelled. Later, another member of her family was buried in Storhøj. The stone bed, thirteen feet long, for a similar coffin had been discovered previously south of her oak coffin, but nothing else had been found; it may have been the burial place of her husband. On the spot where the Egtved girl's coffin stood, a memorial stone has been raised, recording the part played in its discovery by Peter Platz.

The graves of the Egtved girl's family appear now as no more than low banks among the cultivated fields. That she herself was buried in the summertime we know from the flowering yarrow that was found in the coffin, laid with care by her left knee underneath the cow-hide and above the rug. Beneath her lay a frond of bracken.

Yarrow flowers in the summertime. In olden days it was one of the world's most sought-after healing plants and thought to be potent and have magical properties, which made it both a magic herb and an oracular flower. Nowadays it is one of the finest spices known for *snaps*. At the time of the Egtved girl, and even earlier, yarrow was known and honoured in China. For example, the *Book of History*, which begins in 2,357 B.C., records for the thirteenth year of King Wu's reign in the Chou State, in the year 1122, round about the year of the Egtved girl's death: 'Investigation of doubts (questions). Persons who are skilled in prophecy with the aid of tortoise shell and the stalks of the yarrow plant are selected and appointed, after which preparations may be made for the omens to be consulted . . . They will be able to foretell from the portents whether good or evil events are to be expected. Seven omens may be read altogether—five from the tortoise shell and two from the stems of yarrow, whereby errors may be detected.' Yarrow was also one of the most widely used healing plants in the whole of the northern hemisphere in earlier days, and was known to the Greeks and Romans. The Greek doctor Dioscarides called it 'soldier's wort' because soldiers used it for treating wounds and diarrhoea. In France it is known as 'carpenter's wort' because carpenters used it to stop bleeding from cuts, while in England yarrow tea was used

21. The Egtved girl's costume

as a beauty treatment to remove wrinkles and as a cure for
possession by the devil. In Denmark, Henrik Harpestræng
used it, among other things, for treating wounds and to stop
bleeding. It was even included in the Danish pharmacopoeia
right up to the year 1893.

The Mound People, too, may have had good reasons for
laying a head of yarrow flowers in the Egtved girl's coffin. It
lay with its white blossom facing the head of the coffin.
Sometimes yarrow flowers have the same pink tinge as fine
ladies used to have on their cheeks.

It caused quite a sensation when the well-preserved oak
coffin was found at Egtved and its contents were gradually
revealed by the investigation at the National Museum. The
dead woman was immediately christened the 'Egtved girl',
and she has been known as that throughout Denmark ever
since. Accounts of the discovery appeared in the newspapers
with double-column headlines, and it was celebrated in
verse. But when Thomas Thomsen published his painstaking
investigations in a richly illustrated book in 1929, a storm of
indignation broke out. The public had by that time formed a
set image of the Bronze Age woman, in the shape of Madame
Eshøj, with her hair gathered up in a net and her body
covered with a tunic that fitted closely into the top of the
full-length skirt. So when Thomas Thomsen stated that the
Bronze Age woman could also have gone about in a short
tunic—her bare stomach covered only by a small bronze
disc, 'possibly to heighten the effect, like the round breast-
plates of Indian dancers, at once concealing and provocative'
—and a thigh-length skirt, not of closely-woven material but
simply made of cords, and consequently as transparent as the
lace skirts Holberg's Apcius longed to see on the maidens of
1722, their illusions were shattered.

It was too much, even for the not particularly delicate but
very learned Professor Hans Brix: 'And now the costume—
the summer costume. This presents in truth, in itself, a strange
covering for our remarkably moderate and temperate climate;
and its composition is very striking. A cloth tunic—well,

that is a good, warm garment. But the corded skirt: it would have been more sensible and more modest (even by the standards of primitive peoples) if the material had been made into the skirt and the string work—a fish net—used to drape the upper part of the body . . . What, in any case, can the corded skirt have been? Let the learned decide! A sort of underskirt for casual wear; or an indoor garment for use in the over-heated winter hut? A ritual dress?' Thomas Thomsen naturally defended himself, pointing to other finds and to bronze statuettes of Bronze Age women wearing only corded skirts. His picture therefore still holds good: that of a young Bronze Age girl, barely twenty, of medium height, slender and blonde, with a well-groomed appearance and wearing a short-sleeved tunic and a corded skirt to the knees.

But this was not the last time the Egtved girl was to be attacked for her corded skirt, that 'is hardly fit to be called a skirt, being not so much as a covering for her nakedness'. In the 1930s, when the Germans were brimming over with pride at the greatness and virtue of their forefathers, Bronze Age women were always represented with the long skirt down to the ground; but as the corded skirt was, after all, a fact, one could sometimes see it sketched in as an overskirt above the long one!

Fourteen years passed after the Egtved discovery before another of the women of the Mound People came to light. It was on the site of a ruined mound at Skrydstrup, west of Haderslev, in the summer of 1935. The previous year a well-preserved oak coffin had been uncovered a little further north, at Jels, but this merely contained a woollen cap, a leather sandal, a horn comb and three small bronze *tutuli*: it was probably a man's grave, plundered in ancient times.

Whereas the Egtved girl only gave her secrets away little by little as the investigation of her coffin slowly proceeded, the Skrydstrup woman lay there almost completely revealed when she was exposed once more to the light of day after her three-thousand-year sojourn in the burial mound. Her oak coffin had nearly rotted away, the lid having quite disappeared and only a few vestiges of the base remaining. She lay extended on the bed of stones on which the coffin had rested, and was covered by a heap of fist-sized stones that had once been piled above it. Hard-pan between the stones had prevented the water from seeping down and so preserved the dead woman and her clothing in a miraculous manner, even though the heavy oak coffin was almost entirely destroyed.

The National Museum was told of the discovery in a brief letter dated 26th July 1935 from C. M. Lund, director of the Haderslev County Museum: 'This is to inform you that the remains of a coffin burial have been discovered in a mound at Skrydstrup which the museum has been investigating for the past few days. Although the coffin has disintegrated, the whole of the contents, wrapped in woollen material, are still preserved. The find will now be set in plaster of Paris and sent to you for conservation without any attempt to open it.' This was obviously the letter of an experienced museum man and excavator and the further investigations on the spot, the plastering and dispatch, could consequently be left to him in full confidence. C. M. Lund acquitted himself so well that on its arrival at the National Museum, nothing had shifted.

The story of this unique find is as follows. The owner of the mound, which lay close up against his farm and had originally been a very considerable size—thirteen feet high and about seventy-nine feet in diameter—had decided to construct a beet store in it because of its convenient situation. C. M. Lund heard about this, and knowing that two stone platforms containing traces of oak coffins and a bronze sword in each had been found when the southern side of the mound had been excavated in 1931, he obtained the owner's permission to carry out an investigation before any further digging was done. He began on 15th July and this is his account of the excavation: 'We started at the south edge of the mound and when we had worked a good way in, I found a small hole with my stick. I scraped the earth aside and found

22. The Skrydstrup woman on the bed of stones in the burial mound

that the hole was in fact a space between two stones. Then I knew that the mound contained one more grave, in addition to the two that had already been found. We set to and excavated a large square area in the centre of the mound to find that the stones we had encountered first were part of a long bed. This was full of water. We dug a small channel and, when a good many bucketfuls of water had run away, we removed the top stones and then made a sensational discovery. Among the stones, wrapped in a finely-preserved piece of material, lay a body about six feet long.'

It was a piece of sheer good fortune that the original grave came to light so quickly after the mound was first broken into in 1931, and was thereby saved from total destruction. A few years more and nothing but the two gold rings attached to the dead woman's ears would have been found. Everything else would have vanished. The powers that watched over the Mound People had once again kept guard over their dead.

This discovery naturally caused a tremendous stir, and people came from all over the country to see it. On the first Sunday, a couple of thousand came, and during the following days there was such a steady stream of visitors that the removal of the body had to be postponed and a twenty-four hour watch kept over the mound. Finally, admission for visitors had to be restricted to between six and eight in the evening in order to get peace to carry out the necessary measurements and photography. When the work was finished, a large wooden case was constructed round the grave, the boards being carefully inserted one by one under and round the dead woman before they were assembled. Tissue-paper was laid over the contents and all the remaining spaces were filled with plaster of Paris, five hundred pounds of it in all. The find was then ready for removal to Copenhagen, where the exciting investigation could begin.

When the freshly-made lid and the cover of tissue-paper were removed, all that could at first be seen of the woman was the hair on the top of her head. The rest of her was covered with two large pieces of material folded together, through which the shape of her body could be distinguished, marred

23. The Skrydstrup woman undisturbed, and with the rug removed

24. The Skrydstrup woman's head

only by the impress of the stones that had been lying directly on the rug. The dead woman lay on her back with her face tilted upwards and slightly to the left. Her arms rested by her side and her legs were stretched out and drawn slightly together. A glimmer could be caught of the facial features as though seen through an Arabian woman's veil (see the photographs).

As the covering cloths were loosened with care and rolled back, the dead woman materialized fully dressed. That she was a distinguished representative of the womanhood of the Mound People was immediately apparent from the style of hairdressing—the hair was piled high on the head and held with a band over the forehead and a hair-net—the well-shaped face, long and narrow and of Nordic type, and the splendid teeth, the gold rings at the ears, the embroidered tunic and the long skirt, held at the waist with a belt, to which was attached a horn comb in fretted work. After a preliminary scrutiny, but before any closer examination was made, the Skrydstrup girl was exhibited for a few days in the entrance hall of the National Museum, where thousands of visitors had a solemn confrontation with one of their distant ancestors, so miraculously preserved for three thousand years.

After that, a succession of specialists set to work on an exhaustive examination of the Skrydstrup girl herself, her clothing and her other equipment. To give more details, her hair had been piled up high to rest above her forehead on a hair pad, possibly made of her own hair, and covered with a square-meshed hair-net made of black hair from the tail or mane of a horse. The hair was held in place by cords bound several times round the head. The hair of the head was ash blonde with a reddish glint, a little darker over the ears, while the pubic hair was a light reddish-brown. An elaborately woven bonnet made by the 'sprung' technique lay rolled up under her left cheek. An X-ray photograph showed that the brain was still preserved. Rings of gold wire twisted in spirals were coiled round the ears and held in place by the girl's hair which had been drawn through them. The outstandingly beautiful teeth, coated with strong enamel and entirely free

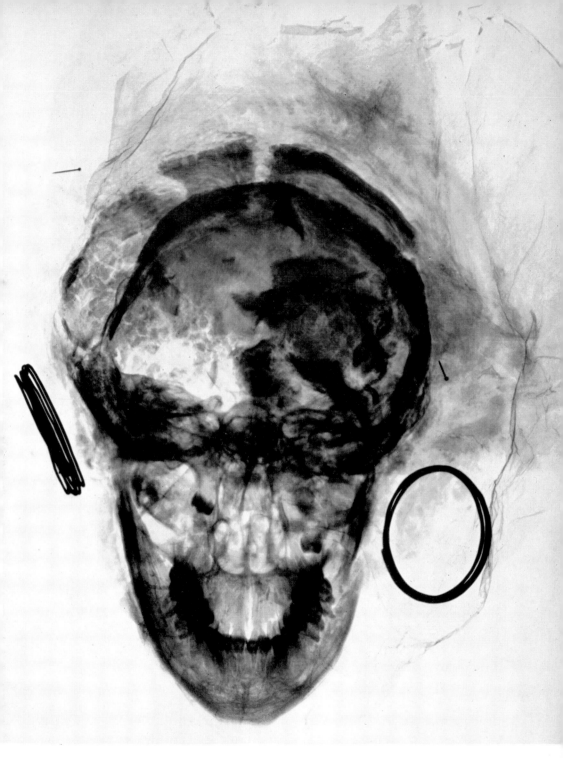

25. X-ray photograph of the Skrydstrup woman's head
    with the gold earrings

from caries or any other dental infection, reveal—with the evidence of the partially preserved arm and leg bones—that she was about eighteen. In build she was tall and slender, being slightly more than five feet seven inches in height.

The dress, made of wool from dark, reddish-brown sheep, and the other textiles were thoroughly examined and described by Margrethe Hald. The short-sleeved tunic was cut in one piece with gussets at the arm-holes and hemmed round the neck with embroidery at the top of the sleeves. The long belt was woven of fine, light-coloured woollen yarn and had a woven fringe at one end but was cut off at the other. It was tied around the long skirt, which completely covered the dead woman including her feet; on these she was wearing a pair of leather moccasins stitched round the edges. Pieces of material were wrapped round the ankles to protect them against chafing by the leather thongs bound round the small of the leg and instep to hold the shoe in place. Inside one of the moccasins were traces of grasses and hair, carefully placed over the sole to make walking more comfortable, just as the Eskimos used to do with their sealskin top-boots.

A remarkable feature was the long skirt, which reached from the waist right down over the feet and was gathered at the top in large folds, held together by the belt. It was made of a number of pieces of material roughly tacked together with a thick thread, measured four feet nine inches by thirteen feet one inch and was cut off down one side without any sort of hem. This unusual size and the bad stitching in comparison with the neatly sewn and embroidered tunic suggested to H. C. Broholm, who did a great deal of work on the finds, that it could not have been a skirt such as the Skrydstrup girl would have worn during her lifetime, but a sort of shroud— like a similarly enormous skirt found in the woman's grave at Borum Eshøj. In this opinion he is supported by the small Bronze Age statuettes of women wearing only corded skirts. Poul Nørlund, however—and later the Swedish expert Bertil Almgren—put forward the theory that the large pieces of material in the women's oak coffins, including the one that covered the Egtved girl, were worn as a whole garment fastened over the shoulders like a *peplos*, which had been the Greek woman's standard garment since the days of Homer, and is known from even earlier times in the eastern Mediterranean area. Conclusive proof for such an assumption is still lacking, but it is not improbable, for during the period of the Mound People there existed trading connections between Scandinavia and Greece. Certainly the spiral ornamentation and the long-prowed Bronze Age ships originated there. The explanation does not preclude the possibility that the long skirts may also have been worn by the women of the Mound People during their daily lives. But nothing except another oak coffin find could decide these questions.

The Skrydstrup girl, too, was buried in the summertime. Under the animal hide that covered her in the coffin— though only a few fragments of it remained at the bottom— lay grasses and the finely serrated leaves of an umbelliferous flower decisively identified by the botanist Johannes Iversen as wood chervil. Remembering the fine aroma which the heads of the yarrow flower, one of which was found in the Egtved girl's coffin, gave to Danish *snaps*, the wood chervil had of course to be tried out too. It produced a delicate flavour and a scent of aniseed, pleasant to those who can take absinthe but, like absinthe, no doubt slightly poisonous. For the rest, it had the same delightful green colour as newly-found bronze objects in the graves of the Mound People.

26. Bronze Age mounds at Resen in Skodborg Hundred

The two archaeologists, whom the finders of the coffin knew from previous work together, Dr Henry Petersen and Captain A. P. Madsen, the museum's incomparable draughtsman, set off straight away for west Jutland and joined in the work of excavation.

A week later Worsaae received another telegram from Ringkøbing:

'PECULIAR COFFIN. MAN OVER 6 FEET. ANIMAL HIDE, CAP, 2 CLOAKS, SHIRT, FOOT COVERING, SWORD, WOODEN SHEATH, BELT BUTTON, HAIR, NAILS, 2 FIBULAE. ALL WELL PRESERVED. AM DIGGING FOR WIFE

HENRY PETERSEN'

The conditions that had preserved the Muldbjerg chieftain for thousands of years were the same as at Egtved and elsewhere: the coffin was packed round with a casing of peat from the fen, still a good four inches thick and containing fragments of heather and moss, greenish in colour, and some birch leaves—but no others.

The oak coffin stood on the base of the mound, embedded in this core of peat on a bed of fist-sized stones which enclosed —like a trough—both the coffin and an enormous hollowed-out oak trunk lying over it like a barrel vault. The great enveloping trunk, rather more than half an oak trunk split lengthwise and hollowed out, still had some of its bark, unlike the coffin itself which was stripped.

When the inner lid was lifted from the coffin, a man's form could be made out, through a layer of hair, with a round cap on his head—as may be seen from A. P. Madsen's drawings. Evidently, the dead man had been wrapped in a cow-hide with the hair side uppermost, but only the hair had survived. Underneath lay two folded articles of clothing, a cape and a rug, which covered him as he lay extended on his back with his head to the north-west at the root end of the coffin. He was wearing a short woollen coat on which rested a bronze sword in a sheath.

Inside the cap was a head of long, dark-coloured hair, swept back and parted in the middle. It had once been fair. All that survived of the head was the lower jaw, as has strangely enough been the case in other graves. Since there was no trace of any beard, the man must have been clean-shaven. On his woollen coat lay two small bronze discs and a fragment of the bone of the right upper arm. Below was the outermost layer of the heavy, black stained leg-bones, ending in two pieces of cloth that had been bound around the feet. A few well-shaped finger-nails from the right hand lay close to the tip of the scabbard.

The unusually well-preserved woollen costume has been examined in detail by H. C. Broholm and Margrethe Hald. It gives a full picture of male dress among the Mound People. The inner garment was a coat thirty-seven inches long,

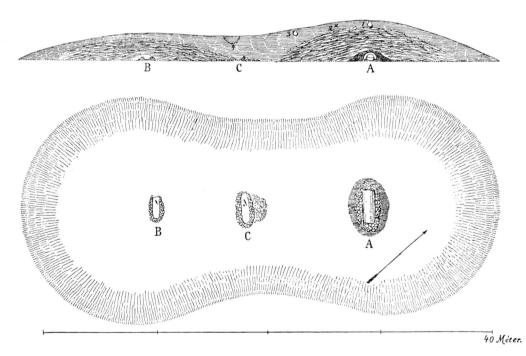

40 Meter.

27. Muldbjerg in section and plan

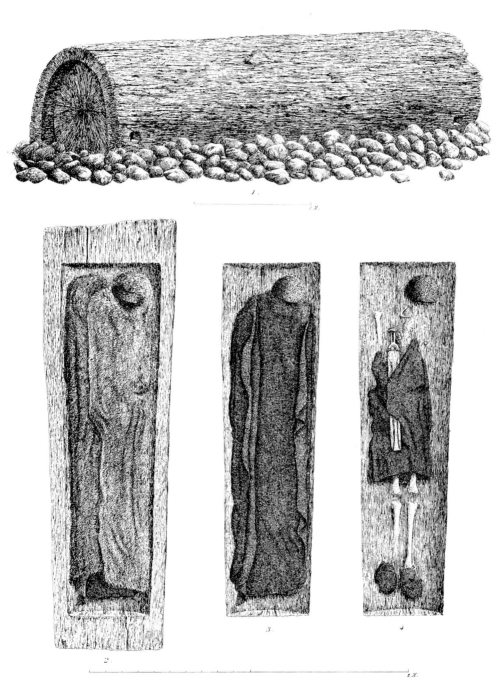

28. The Muldbjerg chieftain's coffin on its bed of stones, and opened

wrapped round the body and fastened over the shoulders with leather straps and the two bronze discs that were lying in the coffin at shoulder level. It was made of nine pieces of material carefully stitched together and overcast, and was designed with a tongue-shaped overlap over the breast. There was a leather belt with a double-headed fastener made of horn at the waist. A knee-length, round-cut, kidney-shaped cape of dark, fulled woollen material had marks of wear on the right side which showed that it had been turned back so that the edge formed a collar and revers. The two round-headed bronze fibulae—the fibula being the safety-pin of the Bronze Age—had been attached to the collar.

The costume was completed by a pair of leather shoes that had disintegrated. All that remained was two long strips of material that had been bound round the ankles to protect them against chafing by the leather thongs holding the shoes on the feet. The circular cap was elaborately constructed, with side-pieces and crown, and consisted of several layers of material. On the inside were sixteen concentric rows of stitching. Externally, it was covered with thousands of short threads, each ending in a knot, so that it had the appearance of a fur cap. It was designed, like a helmet, to protect the head against cuts and blows in battle. The sword that lay on the dead man's chest was carried on a broad leather strap over the shoulder. Marks of wear and tear on the sheath show that it hung at his left side, and that the strap was so long the scabbard scraped the ground.

News of the most recent discovery in Muldbjerg came in a telegram from Ringkøbing dated 17th August 1883:

'EXCAVATION COMPLETED. TWO WOMEN WITH CORRODED DAGGERS, ONE GOLD-MOUNTED. COFFINS OF FIST-SIZED STONES'

Closer investigation revealed the origin of the figure-of-eight ground plan of the mound. Muldbjerg consisted originally of two round burial mounds set side by side. The more northerly one covered the man's grave and the southerly an oak coffin on a bed of stones, on which lay a bronze dagger thirteen inches long with a gold mounting on its pommel and a gold band decorated with 'Mycenaean' spirals about its hilt. Only a thin brownish residual layer remained of the coffin since it had not been packed round with peat, as had the man's grave.

At a later date, another oak coffin was laid on the original surface between these two round burial mounds. It was covered with a smaller mound, so that the three burial mounds merged together to form the 'Mycenaean shield' pattern. In the last grave, too, the sole trace of the oak coffin was a thin brown layer on a trough-shaped bed on stones, where lay a bronze dagger and a belt disc such as we know from the woman's grave in Borum Eshøj. Probably Henry Petersen was right when he announced that he had found 'two women'. On the basis of the structure of Muldbjerg and the contents of the three graves, we may assume that the woman in the south mound died first. After that, the chieftain in the north mound took another wife, but as he died before her, she was finally buried in between the burial mounds erected to him and his first wife. It is naturally possible that the chieftain had two wives, one or both of whom survived him. However, if one takes other oak coffin finds into consideration, the first explanation seems the more probable.

When the excavation was finished, Muldbjerg was thrown up again, restored to its original condition, and declared a protected site. It now lies covered with heather as it was before it revealed the secrets of the Mound People, with wide views westward across Jutland to Stadil Fjord, the sea link with the world from which they fetched their wealth of gold and bronze.

The Muldbjerg burials do not rank among the richest of the two thousand five hundred grave finds known to us from the period of greatness of the Mound People—when the area over which they ruled not merely comprised the whole of Denmark but stretched down through Schleswig and Holstein into Lüneburg and Lower Saxony. It also included the south of Sweden and Norway. The number of coffin burials

F

29. The Muldbjerg chieftain's costume

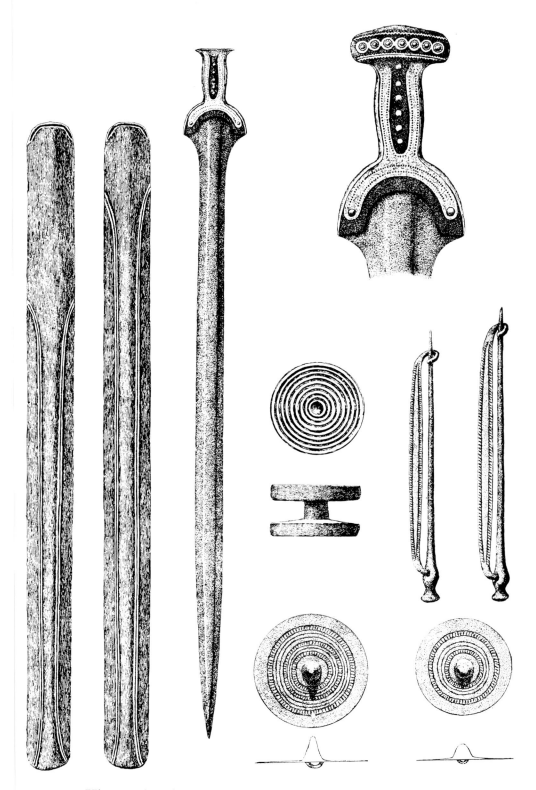

30. His sword and ornaments

'... Mr Herbst and Mr Kornerup would like to start out from here with me immediately after the conclusion of the Scandinavian Students' meeting on Wednesday morning (18th instant), so that we would hope to be in Vamdrup by Thursday evening and start the examination of the coffins immediately afterwards, on the Friday morning.'

The accounts Worsaae submitted to the king, in *rigsdalers*, *marks* and *skillings*, tells us something about the three archaeologists' journey through Denmark and their stay in Vamdrup:

ACCOUNTS
covering

Expenses in connection with the expedition undertaken by myself, Mr Herbst and Mr Kornerup to Vamdrup near Kolding in June 1862 on the gracious instructions of His Majesty the King.

1. Mr Herbst, cab ticket and steamer from Copenhagen to Nyborg	5—3—6
2. Mr Kornerup, ticket from Roskilde to Nyborg	3—4—8
3. Cab for me, ticket and steamer from Copenhagen to Nyborg	5—2—8
4. Breakfast in Ringsted	0—4—2
5. Bridge toll in Nyborg	0—2—6
6. Light refreshments at the same place	0—3—0
7. Special conveyance to Odense with tip	5—2—2
8. Lunch for the Commission	4—4—0
9. Bridge toll. Carriage to Middelfart	8—5—8
10. Supper at the inn	0—4—4
11. Tip for the driver	1—0—0
12. Night's lodging in Middelfart	4—1—8
13. Man at same place	0—2—0
14. Boat to Snoghøj with bridge toll	1—1—0
15. Meal in Snoghøj	0—4—0
16. Special conveyance to Kolding with tip	3—4–12
17. In hotel at the same place dinner etc.	4—5–12

88

18. Carriage to Hjarup and Vamdrup   3—4—2
19. Tips and petty expenses   0—5—8
20. Telegram to His Majesty from Kolding   2—0—0
21. Work people digging for 2 days   7—2—0
22. Lodging and meals for Commission for 2 days 14—0—0
23. Telegram to His Majesty from Aabenraa   1—3—3
24. Carriage to Christiansfeld for Mr Kornerup
      and myself   2—3—0
25. Herbst for packing materials   3—0-14
26. The same for return journey from Vamdrup   19—2—4

Half of hire of carriage and other expenses
for a journey to Fredensborg with the objects
found for His Majesty   8—3—4

Total 115 *R.* 0 *M.* 13 *Sk.*

24th July 1862 Your Majesty's most humble and loyal subject,

J. J. A. WORSAAE

The large mound known as Guldhøj in the group of mounds at Vamdrup was excavated by Vilhelm Boye in the summer of 1891. Originally a very large mound, it had by that time been seriously reduced, having even for a time been completely under the plough. But the three coffins it covered were found in good condition in the core of dark grey, moist sand, which contained thin layers of mosses and mares' tails, twigs of oak and one solitary twig of hazel. The inner mound was entirely enclosed in a layer of hard-pan with an iron content, which had ensured preservation of the highly perishable materials.

Vilhelm Boye writes that he at once encountered a child's coffin measuring four feet three inches, but '. . . I had barely got the coffin cleansed of earth—it took me by surprise, not I it, so that there was no time to telegraph for Madsen—and measured its distance from the outside of the mound and its depth downwards, when a cloudburst overwhelmed us. Within the space of a few minutes the open grave was full of

33. The oak coffin in Guldhøj immediately after opening

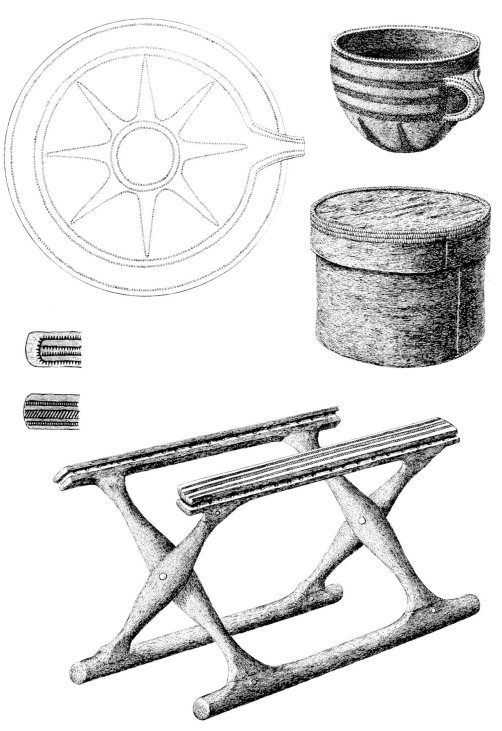

34. A wooden vessel, bark container and folding chair from the
coffin (approx. 1:3)

water and the piled-up earth began to slide down, so that there was nothing to be done but slip ropes round the coffin and raise it with care to the surface; the water was over our knees . . .' When the coffin was opened it was found to have in it no more than faint traces of the dead body in the form of a reddish mass. At the head end lay the lower part of a willow pole and a crab-apple, and at the other two crab-apples. A few remnants of woollen material could be identified, but it was clear that the dead child had been wrapped in a very fine, black-haired goat skin.

Three crab-apples had certainly not been placed in the coffin of one of the Mound People's children without having some special significance. From time immemorial the apple has figured in myth and legend all over the world. It is the fruit of life; and it was with an apple from the Tree of Life in the Garden of Eden that Eve, seduced by the snake, tempted Adam so that they learnt to know good and evil, and were driven out of Paradise. In Crete, the apple was sacred to the lovely Aphrodite, who caused the different kinds of animals to appear and the flowers to spring from the earth. Anyone who was to be sacrificed to the gods there was given an apple to eat, so that he should enjoy eternal life in Elysium—the land 'where human life passes so sweetly and so happily'. The Mound People may well have had the same sort of ideas about the power of the apple as the Cretans, for both used the endless spiral as a symbol on their weapons and ornaments. The three crab-apples in the small coffin in Guldhøj may well have been intended to give the little child a longer life in the next world than the brief one it had had here on earth.

In the middle of the great Guldhøj's base stood a huge sarcophagus, an oak coffin almost ten feet long, covered and surrounded by even longer, roughly-hewn oak planks, still with their original bark on and surrounded by oak chips, which show that possibly both coffins had been made on the spot. A draughtsman drew and measured the coffin and its contents. But he had acquired a dangerous competitor as depicter of antique finds, for Mr Hansen, the headmaster of the school at Vamdrup, arrived on the scene with a new-fangled photographic apparatus with 4 x 6 inch plates from Craftint of Ohio and took the pictures that are reproduced here. Vilhelm Boye wrote a little anxiously from Vamdrup to Copenhagen: 'I do not know whether I should order a set of photographs for the museum (35 Øre each, mounted).'

The coffin contained magnificent furnishings, although of the dead chieftain himself nothing but the short fair hair and the brain remained. The weapons and clothing showed the grave to be that of a man. He lay under a cow-hide in the usual costume of the Mound People: a round cap worked all over with loose threads, a coat with a woven belt, and leather shoes laid under his head like a pillow, covered by his cape. Another cap was found in the folds of the cape at the head of the coffin, with parts of a cloth mitten made in the same way as those of the Iglulik Eskimos and the Naskapi Indians. A bronze battle-axe, hafted in an ash wood shaft, lay by his left shoulder, and in the centre of the coffin was a bronze dagger in a wooden scabbard. There was also a bronze fibula, various fragments of leather and six split hazel sticks, cut off at the ends, measuring from two and a half to three and three quarter inches in length. At the foot of the coffin was a large bowl carved out of the root of an ash tree and inside it a smaller one of birch wood—both with handles and ornamented with tin pins arranged in a star pattern. In addition, there was a lidded bark container, stitched with strips of osier, and a folding chair of ash wood with the remains of a seat of otter skin. This remarkable article was found without the nails that would have held it together; but nails from similar chairs are known from other finds, which shows that the chair was a valued piece of furniture. Folding chairs of the same type are known from contemporary finds and representations in the eastern Mediterranean in Greece, Crete and Egypt, and show how far-flung was the world of which the Mound People's culture was a part.

What the six split and cut hazel sticks meant, lying with the dagger where the belt would have gone, we do not know; but the hazel tree was one of 'the nine kinds of wood' that were ingredients in various witchcraft cures in popular medicine, and was also used as a divining-rod, to locate metal among other things. A hazel stick bound about with strips of skin was found, together with other magical objects, in a leather case in an oak coffin grave in Garderhøj at Lyngby— a burial that will be discussed later. In medieval allegories of the southern countries the hazel was honoured as the symbol of rebirth, the nut being the kernel from which new life springs. The hazel stick was found in the shape of a cross in a Viking Age chamber grave under Hørning church on Djursland; the hazel symbolized life. The faith the Vikings and the early Christians placed in it may be of ancient origin in Denmark.

Guldhøj also held another oak coffin close to that of the child. It was in unusually good condition and was formed of an oak trunk eight feet ten inches long and carefully stripped of its bark, standing on the original ground surface. It was supported by three hazel trunks six feet seven inches long, bound together with bast, on one side, and a similar support on the other. Holes had been cut in the ends of the coffin and squared-off, and pointed oak poles thrust through them and driven down into the base of the mound kept the coffin in place—forming a construction that is known from oak coffins already mentioned (see page 84).

Wilhelm Boye had high expectations of this coffin and sent for Captain A. P. Madsen to be his draughtsman. 'Unfortunately, the yield today from the fine, large coffin was a bitter disappointment', wrote Boye, one 'Saturday evening 18/7/91' to the Museum, continuing: 'A hole had been cut in the lid at one end, larger than the hole in the Barde coffin. I realized at once that something was wrong, and it turned out that the grave had been so thoroughly plundered that, apart from a few scraps of skin and traces of woven woollen material, all that survived was one miserable flat double-headed fastener, apparently of horn. At the side of the coffin (*outside* the coffin) lay a hooked stick, which the vandals had presumably used.'

There can be no doubt that the two feet two inch long

94

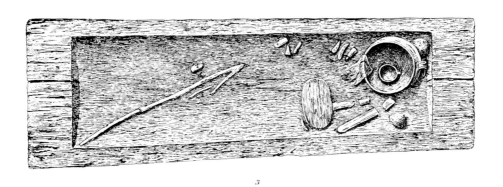

35. The oak coffin from Barde Store Høj, showing the hole
made by the thief

hazel stick with its one and three quarter inch hook, lying beside the coffin, was at the same time the thief's working tool and his 'divining-rod for pointing the way to metals', for this tool, certainly one of the oldest and most primitive of its kind, is also known from another find. That the plundering took place not long after the burial is shown by, amongst other things, the layer of hard-pan that had formed over the coffins and preserved them before decomposition set in. Bronze swords and gold rings were unquestionably far more valuable then than at any later period.

The other definite proof of plundering during the Bronze Age itself had been revealed some ten years previously in 1882, when Barde Store Høj was excavated. This mound stands in the western part of central Jutland, at the confluence of the rivers Abild and Vorgod, which flow southwards until they join the river Skjern that carries their waters out into Ringkøbing fjord—a course which was also the Mound People's way to the ocean in the west. The well-grown oak coffin was in such good condition that the grooves —one to two inches wide—cut by the chisels that hollowed it out could clearly be seen, as well as marks of the wedges with which the green tree-trunk was split. But four feet seven inches from the foot end was a sinister hole, five inches by eight inches across, in the otherwise well-preserved lid. Through this hole the coffin had partially filled with sand. Underneath, at the very bottom, lay a stick two feet nine inches long, on which a side branch formed a long hook. One of the things that the thieves had fished out of the coffin with it was revealed by the presence of a scabbard without a sword. That it had been a rich grave is shown by what was left: an ornamented gold band, a pair of tweezers and a bronze belt-fastener. An oval bark container may have held three flaked flint tools, a few sticks of wood held together by osiers, a wooden haft for a bronze awl and a small wooden handle for a similar implement.

These small objects may indicate that the dead person was a 'medicine man'. In the furthest corner of the coffin, beyond the reach of the thief's hook, stood a fine wooden vessel,

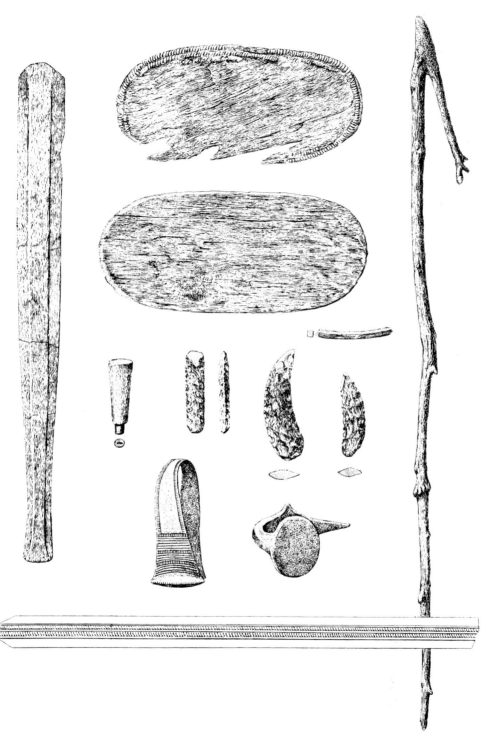

36. The thief's hooked stick and what he left behind in
Barde Store Høj

decorated with a star pattern in tin pins and holding a smaller wooden cup. Of the dead man himself all that was left was a couple of fragments of the brain, and, of his clothes, a shred of woollen material.

The hooked sticks in Guldhøj and Barde Store Høj doubtless explain why it is that in so many Bronze Age burial mounds all that remains on the bed of stones where the coffin rested, is a thin brownish residual layer, with not a vestige of the dead person's funeral furnishings. Presumably such graves were plundered in the time of the Mound People. Grave robbing is known all the world over, and these plunderings often took place at a time when it was still known what treasures the grave held. That applies, for example, to the Egyptian pyramids and shaft graves, the largest of Bahrain's hundred thousand burial mounds, the Norwegian Viking ship burials, the Danish Viking ship grave at Ladby and the Royal Mound at Jelling. The plunderer's tool in the Mound People's grave tells us how valuable a bronze sword was at the time. But gold, too, was to be found in the oak coffins: finger rings, arm rings and earrings of gold wire—as in the Skrydstrup grave—twisted arm rings of heavy gold (encountered most frequently in a man's grave), gold-mounted fibulae and belt-fasteners. Some five hundred gold articles of this sort found in the oak coffin graves of Denmark speak of a people rich in gold.

5 · The Sun and the Horse

MANY finds bear witness to the fact that the sun was the Mound People's deity. Outstanding among them is the figure of the sun in gold and bronze drawn by the sacred horse that was found at Trundholm in north-west Zealand. It came to the surface one September day in 1902 at the first ploughing of a patch of bog which opens out in the west to the wide Sejerø bay, and is enclosed to the north and east by a range of hills crowned by hundreds of Bronze Age mounds.

The bronze horse was the first thing to be thrown up. It appeared head foremost and was immediately noticed and picked up. On the return journey, the sun disc came to light in the next furrow, just opposite the spot where the horse had been found. It, too, was picked up, together with various pieces of bronze lying scattered in the furrows, but no systematic search was made. The ploughman simply marked the place with a couple of twigs and took the objects to his home, where they were put in the loft for the children to play with. But many people heard about the remarkable finds and came to see them. About a week after, news of them reached Mr P. West, the forestry treasurer, who went at once to the farm and was allowed to take the objects into his care, informing the National Museum—which quickly sent someone to Trundholm to look at the spot more carefully.

Trundholm is a raised area in the bog and stands about three feet higher than the surrounding ground, which is drained to the west by Fugle brook. The layer of bog on

99

37. The gold vessel from Mariesminde

Trundholm was only a foot and a half thick and rested on the ancient seashore of the Kitchen Midden period. The search led to the finding, partly in the ploughed-up bog soil and partly deeper down in a mass of firm, moist peat, of rolled-up fragments of gold plating from the sun disc and parts of various bronze wheels, all within a radius of about a yard from the spot where the horse and sun disc had been ploughed up. It proved possible, in spite of their broken condition, to reassemble the pieces with certainty into an almost complete ensemble: a bronze horse drawing a bronze disc, gold-plated on one side—the whole set on a base of three pairs of bronze wheels.

The bronze disc was 10·2 inches in diameter and was constructed from two convex plates held together and encircled by a heavy outer ring. Both were covered with incised designs of concentric rings in oblique lines or angles, set in three bands with, between them, ornamentation in circles of diminishing size which, on the side that was not gold-plated, took the form of a continuous spiral. This kind of ornamentation is to be found on hundreds of weapons and ornaments belonging to the Mound People, which bear the same symbols as the sun disc; it shows that they were the work of the same skilful bronze-smiths as made the sun disc. One side alone of the bronze disc is now covered with very thin gold-plate—held firmly along the edge by a copper thread hammered down into a groove. The leaf-thin gold was pressed so tightly against the bronze disc that the ornamentation shows through, but the lines were also scored with a pin-point to make them stand out better. The outer edge of the bronze plate was marked with parallel lines set close together to form a halo—not present on the side without the gold overlay, though it too must also have been intended to have the same gold design since it has the same groove and copper thread hammered into it. However, there is no trace of it.

The hollow-cast bronze horse is a distinctive and impressive work of art, unique of its kind. Contemporary parallels are nowhere to be found except in Greece. It is a highly bred animal, smooth and well rounded, with head

38. The sun drawn by the sacred horse, from Trundholm: day and night sides (approx. 1 : 4)

and ears pointing forwards and the tail, which was originally somewhat longer than it is now, projecting backwards. The eyes are represented by convex stars, while line ornamentation marks out the mane and harness. At the front of the neck are the remains of an opening through which the cord would have passed that attached the horse to the sun disc—which has a corresponding opening on the edge nearest the horse.

The Trundholm group represents the sun drawn by a horse since it is also shown in one or two rock engravings in Bohuslän in Sweden. The addition of wheels to the Trundholm sun and its horse, which are not to be seen in the rock engravings, was to make them mobile for the occasions when the priest-chief had to lead them round at the ceremonies at which the sun was worshipped as a god. Possibly the image was a copy of a larger one carved in wood that might have been borne on a cart at the sun festivals to ensure happiness and fertility to man and beast.

The shining, gold side of the disc with the halo design is interpreted as representing the bright sun of day that was drawn from east to west—from left to right across the vault of heaven—while the dark, bronze side is the extinguished sun drawn by night by underground ways to a fresh dawn in the east. The idea of the horse-drawn sun on the blue fields of heaven is of Indo-European origin and is known from pre-Indian and early Greek mythology. An echo of it is found two thousand years later in Viking mythology which tells of Skinfakse, the horse with the shining mane, who draws the light of day each morning across the world of man.

That the sun chariot from Trundholm was not the only one of its kind at the time is shown, among other things, by a large find from Tågaborg Mound in Helsingborg. This was broken to pieces when it was brought out in 1895. All that could be salvaged was three oxen, three spearheads and two small horses, all of bronze. The two horses probably drew a sun image, for it was stated that the find also included 'parts of a small waggon and a bronze disc the size of the blade of a spade'.

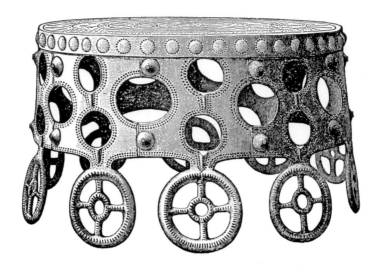

39. The sun drum from Balkåkra (approx. 1 : 5)

r
v
b
t
i
w
K
fo
th
ol
an
ex
ag
ab
sc
in
th
be
pe

wh
by
mo
for
sou
Bre
but
hac

F
fan
of t
of a
Pro
beer
trad
of tl
ridi
idea

40. Bredhøj seen from the north

42. Picture stones on the north side of the Kivik coffin

away as the Mediterranean, where similar carvings are known
—in the shaft graves at Mycenae in the Peloponnese and on
the Hagia Triada sarcophagus in Crete, among other places.

Of the eight lateral stones of the coffin, the four of nearly
equal size are carved: two with scenes of action, the others
with symbolic figures representing the sun, the moon and
other heavenly deities. All the carved surfaces are framed with
a single or double line, a feature unique to the art of the
Bronze Age. This framing gives the carved surfaces the
appearance of painted tapestry, which might even have
been their inspiration.

On the six stones, the symbols of the wheel cross, axes and
horses and other signs are arranged symmetrically two by two,
but the symmetry is broken on the two stones representing
funeral ceremonies where the scenes follow in three rows
one below another. On the southernmost stone, beside the
entrance, there is a rounded shape with an ear, and below
that, from left to right (the way the carvings run), two men
blowing *lurs* (trumpets), next a man holding a square object
in his raised hand, then two men beating a hanging drum, the
whole sequence being surrounded by a circular line which a
figure dressed in a coat is holding onto. The central space is
dominated by a large vessel or altar, towards which two
groups of five and three birdlike people in ankle-length
clothing respectively are facing. In the bottom row, two
groups of four people stand at the entrance to a circular room.
In each group, three of the men are armless—it looks as
though their hands are tied behind their backs—while the
fourth holds a drawn sword in his hand.

Some of the same characters appear again on the next
stone, the second from the entrance on the west side of the
coffin. Three men with their hands tied behind their backs
and a fourth with a raised sword stand in front of a two-
wheeled horse-drawn war chariot, driven by a charioteer.
Underneath in the next row is depicted a stallion fight, a fish
figure and possibly a dog. The shrouded, birdlike figures of the
first stone form the bottom row and move in procession
towards a man who holds a square object in his hand and is

43. The second picture stone on the north side of the Kivik coffin

therefore the same as the person who stands in front of the men blowing the *lurs* on the first stone.

The ceremonies held in honour of the dead chief at his funeral were thus many and varied: the blowing of *lurs*, the beating of drums, chariot races, stallion fights, human sacrifices and processions of men shrouded in long garments. These significant events were given enduring power by being carved into the lateral stones of the grave, together with the protective signs of the heavenly deities and the ship that was to carry the chieftain and his retinue to the kingdom of the dead beyond the sea.

When we spoke above of the guardian of the sun image from Trundholm fen as one of the priest-chieftains of the Mound People—a *gode* (boon, advantage) as priests were called in the Viking Age—this was because gold discs similar to that of the Trundholm sun have been found in a number of graves. One was taken from a mound in Jægersborg Hegn, the central grave of which—a disintegrated oak coffin covered by a heap of stones—contained some splendid pieces of male equipment: sword, axe, belt-attachment, small bronze discs, and a clay vessel. In the centre of the coffin above the sword lay an ornamented bronze disc overlaid with a thin sheet of gold, fourteen and a quarter inches across, considerably larger than the Trundholm disc. It had in the centre a sun casting out rays and surrounded by rings set close together to the very edge of the disc.

Another gold sheet attached to the remains of a bronze disc, found with a bronze sword in the centre of a coffin in Solhøj at Sønder Tranders in north-west Himmerland, is about the same size—roughly thirteen inches across. Of two oak coffin graves, which had almost completely vanished, in a mound at Tødsø on Mors, one was empty while the other contained a man's equipment of sword, dagger and two fibulae, with a paper-thin gold disc in addition, about thirteen inches in diameter, that had presumably been mounted once on a bronze disc decorated with concentric rings. It lay on top of the sword and dagger in the centre of the grave.

Certain burials containing strange articles, over and above

H

items normally found in graves, that have only been used for witchcraft and magic, or as amulets, testify to the power of Bronze Age chieftains in matters that go beyond day-to-day existence.

One such discovery was made in 1886 in one of the largest burial mounds in Denmark, the mighty Løfthøj, also known as Gardehøj, at Jægersborg, north of Copenhagen. It was almost twenty-three feet high and 108 feet across, and built of turfs that had been lifted in large slabs. At the base lay the remains of an oak coffin packed round with a thick layer of eel-grass and covered with a heap of stones. Only faint traces of the dead man remained, but it could be seen that the sword had rested on his breast and a huge, twisted gold ring had been on his left wrist. Beside the scabbard, on the breast over his heart, lay a leather bag, a double-headed bronze fastener attached to a strap, and a bronze pin nearly seven inches long with which the bag had been fastened. Inside the largely disintegrated bag was found a small bronze knife with a crooked blade, a broken razor, a pair of tweezers, a stick of wood wrapped round with strips of skin, two leather cases bound with string and a very sharp flaked flint blade, stitched up in leather.

Another similar find was made in a burial mound on Hvidegård Farm in the parish of Kongens Lyngby, a mere half mile north of Løfthøj. A letter from Count Trampe, dated Sorgenfri Castle, 14th August 1845, to the Museum of Northern Antiquities stated that 'a man in Lyngby has today found an undamaged giant grave. A sword can be seen sticking out from under the large top stone'. The Director of the Museum, the famous Chr. Jürgensen Thomsen, was on the spot the next day, but owing to a heavy rainstorm and lack of 'the necessary apparatus' the investigation proper could not take place until 19th August.

This time Thomsen was accompanied by the assistant keepers, Strunk and Herbst, and Ibsen, a regimental surgeon. In a stone coffin, the bottom of which was covered with small flints, lay an animal skin with the hair side outermost on which were the dead man's clothes, a cape and a coat—

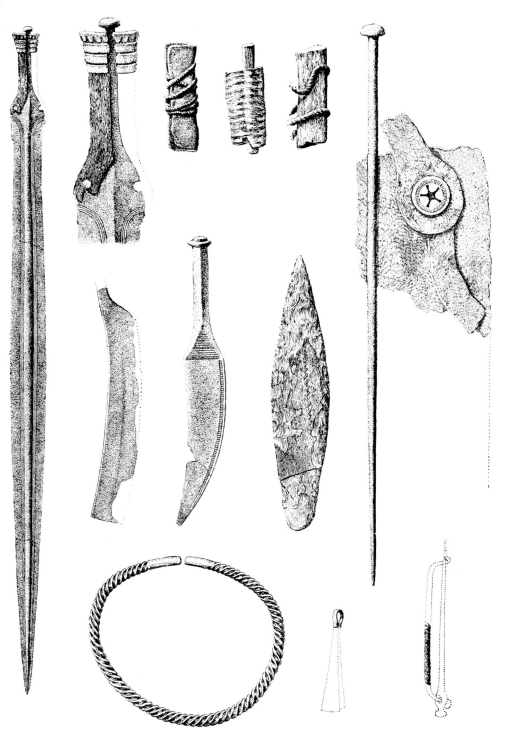

44. The Løfthøj chieftain's sword, gold ring and magic charms

from the edge of which protruded a sword in its scabbard and sword-belt. Among the woollen material lay a heap of burnt bones of an adult male, a fibula and a leather bag. This bag was closed with a bronze pin, like the one from Løfthøj, thrust through a row of leather eyelets so that it could be opened or closed by simply pulling a leather strap attached under the head of the pin. It was the Mound People's brilliant discovery of the zip-fastener.

Inside the bag were the most extraordinary objects: a piece of amber bead, a small conch shell—and a broken piece of a larger one—a small cube of wood, a flint flake, a number of different dried roots, a piece of bark, the tail of a grass-snake, a falcon's claw, a small, slender pair of tweezers, a bronze knife in a leather case, a razor with a horse's head handle in a case bound with a thin leather thong, a small flint knife stitched into an intestine or bladder, a small, inch-and-a-half-long leather case in which there was the lower jaw of a young squirrel and a small bladder or intestine containing several small articles. Herbst was by now fairly certain that the contents of the bag had been used for 'sorcery or witchcraft' and had in fact belonged to a medicine man.

Belt bags with similar contents are known from at least thirty Bronze Age graves throughout the country. The best equipped of all was found recently in a mound at Egtved. It had in it no less than twenty-three articles, among them a bronze sickle, the remains of a comb, an awl and a sewing needle stuck into a twist of wool, scraps of bronze and amber, a strip of leather (?) tied round with string, a piece of nut-shell, a piece of charcoal and two pieces of mica.

The Mound People can have had no doubts that the priest-chieftains, with the help of their amulets, had power over sickness and hidden dangers. How and for what purposes the many different things had been used, we do not know, but faith in amulets for bringing happiness or warding off evil, and in their powers of healing and witchcraft, persist to the present day and may perhaps have their roots in the Bronze Age.

Some of the knives of flint and bronze that have been found

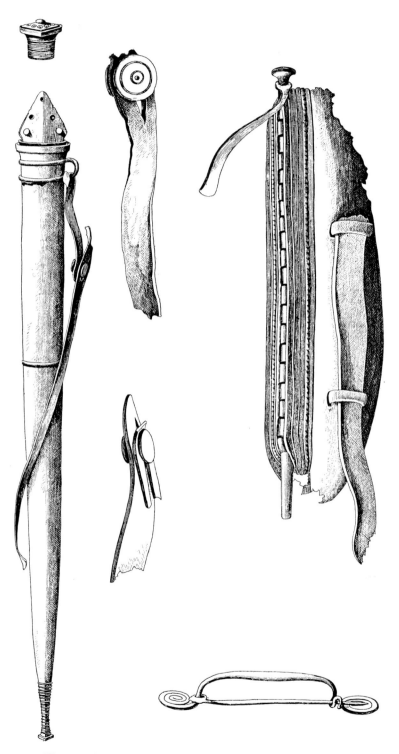

45. The Hvidegård chieftain's sword, fibula and bag with
    zip-fastener

in the leather bags may have been used—practical purposes apart—for surgical operations such as, for example, trepanning, the operation on the brain, which was known even in the Stone Age and is still a life or death operation. A Bronze Age grave containing a trepanned skull was investigated in 1840 by the owner of Lundtofte farm, Hartvig Duncan, who published in the same year a little book on his observations during the excavation. As Duncan had been in need both of marl for his land and stones for road building, he had started digging into a levelled mound lying only about a mile and a quarter north of the Hvidegård mound. A short bronze sword unexpectedly came to light in a heap of stones, after which the workmen proceeded more cautiously until they came upon an unusually well-preserved skeleton in a grave lying deeper down in the sand marl under the mound. Beside the head lay a bronze knife that had almost disintegrated, having been eaten away by the lime in the soil, which had at the same time totally preserved the bones—they had a reddish colour: 'The teeth were gleaming white and extremely strong, the forehead rather protruding, and the bone behind the eyebrows seemed to me the same,' writes Duncan. Later on in his account, he continues: 'There was one circumstance about the skull that seems to me highly remarkable. Immediately after the discovery, I noticed that the upper part of the head or crown had been cut off by a very regular incision. This segment was not present in the grave, and cannot have decomposed or rotted away as the other bones were completely sound; but not the faintest trace of the missing piece was present in the white sand in which the head actually lay, for I myself was present the whole time, and searched most carefully.' The skull was examined some fifty years later by an Army doctor, Søren Hansen, who wrote in an article, 'On Prehistoric Trepanning in Denmark', that whereas two trepannings of skulls from Stone Age graves had had successful outcomes, the patients living for many years after the operations, the Lundtofte man died at once. He says of the trepanning: 'The upper part of the incision turns slightly outwards all along, forming a sharp angle with

the inner surface of the skull and giving the impression that
the surgeon was trying to direct the incision in such a way
that it would have a sideways impact on the surface of the
brain and so avoid damaging it. As an operation executed in
this manner became very much more difficult and prolonged
than if the incision was made more vertically onto the surface
of the brain, it strongly suggests that the operation was
conducted on the patient with full awareness of the great
danger inherent in any trepanning operation.' Even if the
Lundtofte man did not survive the operation, the method
used on this occasion was the same as that employed in
similar operations that were successful and gave the patient
prolonged life.

The Mound People's golden age, as evidenced in the oak
coffins, possibly lasted a mere hundred years—that is, four
to five generations—during the period round about the year
1250 B.C. It is the second of the six great periods into which
the thousand years of the Bronze Age from about 1,500 B.C.
to 500 B.C., is divided. At that time, as has been pointed out
above (see page 81), not only the whole of Denmark and
southern Sweden but also south Schleswig and Holstein, all
of Mecklenburg, west Pomerania, Rügen and parts of
Brandenburg north of the rivers Havel and Spree were united
in one huge cultural area. So firmly rooted was the Bronze Age
culture in Scandinavia that it persisted there for nearly five
hundred years longer than it did in central Europe, where the
Iron Age was to set in earlier, in spite of the fact that steady
trade communications and powerful influences were little by
little altering its character completely. This perhaps more
than anything else indicates the inner strength of the Scandinavian Bronze Age culture.

The background to the Danish Bronze Age must be sought
in the migrations of the Stone Age when, five hundred years
before, the Battle-axe people penetrated westwards into
central and northern Europe. Their homeland lay far to the
east, on the further side of the river Volga in the mountainous
steppe-lands that continue uninterrupted into central Asia—
where there developed in the fourth millennium B.C. a nomadic

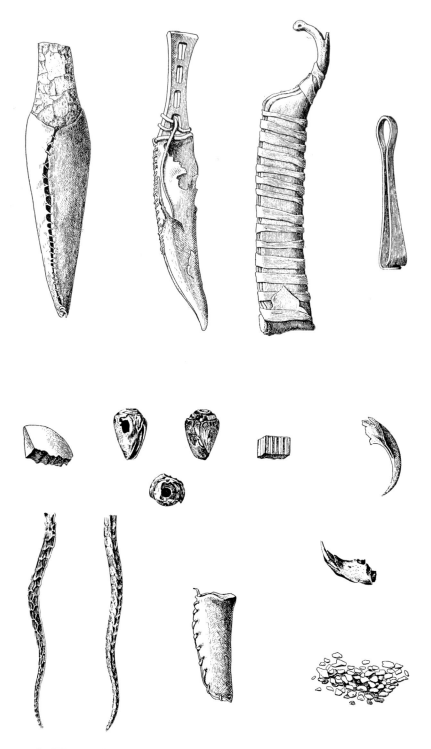

46. The Hvidegård chieftain's magic charms

cattle-breeding culture of enormous extent. In the course of the fourth and third millennia, the climate in these distant parts grew steadily warmer. Since the rainfall decreased at the same time, the grass-covered plains on which the nomadic peoples kept their animals and their tents turned to arid steppe that gradually became less and less capable of providing sufficient food for the vast numbers of horses, oxen, sheep and goats they had. One tribe after another broke away in long caravans, led by horsemen, to seek fresh pastures in other parts of the world. The 'Indo-Europeans' left their homelands and scattered in every direction. Whereever they went, they spread amazement and terror, for in most places no one had ever seen men on horseback. In the Indus valley, they destroyed an advanced urban culture and large, well-ordered communities. In Egypt, they made themselves masters over most of the country in rather less than two centuries. Their kings rose to be Pharaohs and appropriated to themselves the ancient culture of Egypt. They were driven out in about the year 1,600 B.C. by Aahmes I. Their gift to Egyptian culture was the horse and chariot. In Greece, the horseman was interpreted as half-horse, half-man, and was preserved in myth as the centaur, whose wildness and craving for women and wine roused fear and wonder.

Many tribes settled during the long journey through central Russia, Poland and central Europe, along the Baltic coast and through southern Sweden. The battle-axe was their favourite weapon and always accompanied them to the grave. In Jutland, the Battle-axe people immediately subjugated the great river valleys of western Jutland, the Gudenå valley and the smaller valleys that run into it. Kindred tribes operating from bases along the south and west coasts of the Baltic subsequently occupied the islands, east Jutland and Vendsyssel. But the Battle-axe people who settled in Denmark maintained constant communications with their fellow-tribesmen in other countries. Influences from such distant people as the Hittites who settled in Asia Minor—their kingdoms flourishing there in the second millennium B.C.—

47. The northern of the two Stabelhøje on Mols,
    seen from the south

may be traced as far as the Scandinavian Bronze Age areas.

From the wide plains of Asia, where the heavenly powers watched over the fortunes of these nomadic peoples and the fertility of their animals, the Battle-axe people brought the sun as deity and the horse as his draught animal to Scandinavia. At the time of the Mound People the sun was the supreme power worshipped. Later it was displaced to some extent by other gods, but it never quite disappeared. The ancient belief in the sun and the horse can be traced to comparatively modern times. Gutorm Gjessing believes, for instance, that the small horse forming a handle to the mangling boards which young countrymen gave their sweethearts in the eighteenth and nineteenth centuries as betrothal gifts, and which were used for mangling linen, may be the last descendant of the Trundholm horse, and that the cross sign carved on the upper surface of the board was the sun symbol. Admittedly, the earliest mangling boards have no horse, but it may be due to the fact that they were introduced from the towns where the horse had long been forgotten as a symbol. In the country, the horse still survived as a symbol of fertility: the handle which the betrothed girl would hold as she mangled her linen was shaped like a horse to ensure fertility in the coming marriage. In the latter part of the Bronze Age, the horse and sun—or sun symbol—were constantly represented, while in the Iron Age the horse continued to play a large part as a sacrificial animal selected for the purpose by stallion fights, as represented on artifacts and carvings.

The sun was worshipped on the highest hills in the country. One of these is Borgbjerg at Boeslunde between Skelskør and Korsør. That this 'bjerg' or hill was a sacred place in the Bronze Age is revealed by valuable objects recovered from its slopes. The first discovery was made by Maren Paulsdatter Quistgaard during the ploughing in 1842 when the ploughshare threw up two magnificent gold bowls on the northern side. The men dug in search of more but all they found was charcoal and ashes at a rather lower level. Maren's husband, Jeppe Karstensen, who was a tenant farmer, was able to buy his farm with the 454 *rigsdaler* he received as a reward for the bowls. With the prosperity the find had brought the family, Jeppe Karstensen's son, Jens Jeppesen, was able to study as a veterinary surgeon and he afterwards became the head of an agricultural school, taking Borgbjerg as his surname. His sons were the doctor Axel Borgbjerg and the well-known politician Frederik Jeppesen Borgbjerg, who started his career as a writer with a letter to the newspaper *Social-Demokraten* in 1890, signed 'A Peasant Student', and ended up as Minister of Education. It was Bronze Age gold that raised this family from rags to riches.

In May 1874, gold was once again found on Borgbjerg, this time in the shape of two gold cups and two scoops with horse's-head handles. 'They formed a square', the two cups lying close together and the two scoops facing one another.

The glorious repoussé gold vessels known from some ten different finds in Denmark came from a long way off, made as they were in various places in central Europe and not having been introduced into Denmark until the time of the Mound People. Many of them bear the sign of the wheel on their base—to the Mound People the symbol of the sun. Some were therefore provided with horse's-head handles and transformed into figures of the horse and the sun, like the one from Trundholm.

The largest find of gold vessels with horse's-head handles was made in June 1862 by a poor smallholder who had been given permission to cut peat on a farmer's land in Maries-minde Fen at Rønninge, between Odense and Svendborg. Eleven gold bowls had been placed inside a large bronze vessel with their handles downwards. Other gold vessels have been found under large stones or placed inside clay vessels as sacrifices to the gods.

That Borgbjerg was a place of sacrifice is shown by the two gold finds and by the strange terraces that were cut into its sides, as was mentioned in connection with the appearance of the first find. The bank was then a regular square, measuring about 328 feet from north to south and a little more from east to west, and barely sixty-five feet in height. Two terraces about eleven and a half feet wide, running all the way round divided it into three roughly equal sections so that Borgbjerg at that time resembled the structures known in Mesopotamia as ziggurats, built in the third millennium before Christ as the foundations for temple buildings.

The ancient sacred hill at Boeslunde is now badly ravaged. Some traces of the old terraces may still be seen to the south, and something of the original flat top remains. But the hill has been eroded on all sides by gravel quarries and buildings have crept up close beside it. It has now been converted into a memorial garden for F. J. Borgbjerg. Even so, the site is worth a visit. It lies there like a broad brow exposed to the sky and the sun—two of the Mound People's most powerful divinities. From the top, one has a magnificent view over south-west Jutland, the Great Belt and the Småland Sea across to the distant coasts of Funen and Langeland. The unusually large brick church of Boeslunde, dating from about 1300, lies immediately east of Borgbjerg, over the top of which the windows of its tower look out to sea. It is called the Church of the Holy Cross and was a place of pilgrimage. Between it and Borgbjerg is the miraculous well, the Spring of the Holy Cross, that was widely famed in the Middle Ages for its healing qualities, and was attributed with miraculous powers in the time of the Mound People, too. Nowadays, people go to the public house on the other side of the road.

The Trundholm sun chariot is our prime testimony to the fact that sun worship was practised among the Mound People. But why was this splendid work of art broken and buried on a peat-grown island in a fen? Possibly it was done in a particularly rainy period when man and beast and the very ground longed so much for sun that the best things they possessed had to be sacrificed in order that the god should send his blessed light over the land once more. At the sacrifice the glorious image of the sun was broken and 'killed' to give it eternal life in the keeping of the sun god.

6 · The Ox, the Ship, the Plough

OF the dwellings of the Mound People we have little knowledge, although we know their graves by the thousand and
have found their magnificent bronze objects buried in bog
and earth as sacrifices to the gods they worshipped. There
must be special reasons for this, for houses and dwellings are
known in considerable numbers from both the Stone Age and
the succeeding Iron Age periods. In fact, it seems probable
that the distinguished and aristocratic Mound People lived in
quite impressive wooden buildings, a number of houses being
gathered together as in the large Norwegian farms of the last
century. But this type of dwelling leaves few traces in the
ground after the passage of three thousand years. One day the
dwellings will certainly turn up, covered by a relatively thin
cultural stratum—for the saying is: the thinner the cultural
stratum, the higher the culture. The first suggestion of a house
has already been found in Baller fen near Jægerspris on
Zealand. But the ground plan which lay partially covered by
an early Bronze Age mound measured only ten by eleven and
a half feet. Since the building had no fireplace, it must have
been a mortuary house associated with the burial cult.

The assumption that the Mound People lived in wooden
buildings is based on the testimony of the numerous oak
coffins to their skill in woodwork; they could both fell and
hollow out heavy oak trunks and split off planks. Many of the
details show a high degree of craftsmanship. Some of the
coffins have handles, and others holes cut into the ends
through which carefully shaped oak stakes were driven so

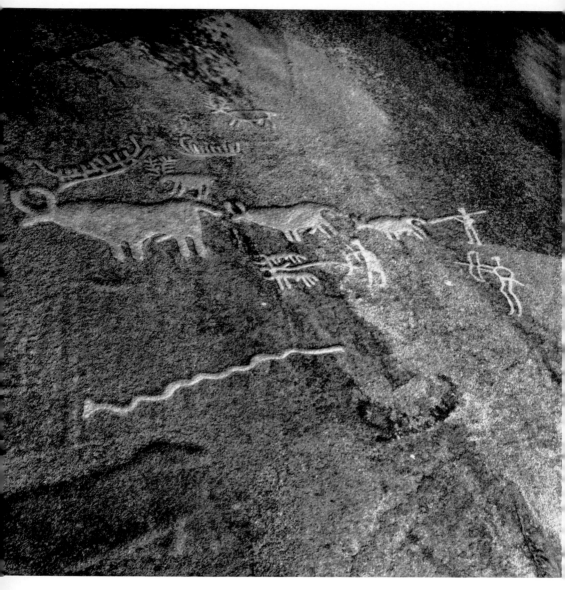

48. Rock-carving from Aspeberget in Bohuslän

that the coffins would stand firmly on the base of the mound without further support. A yardstick that was evidently a Bronze Age carpenter's rule was found at Borum Eshøj, as we saw in Chapter 2 (page 38).

A small number of mortuary houses are known from the most southerly area occupied by the Mound People, round the Lower Elbe. These were erected on the site of the mound, burnt down in the course of the ceremonies associated with the funeral, and finally covered by the mound. Those found have mostly been smallish wattle and post structures with a pitched roof. An exception is a 'megaron house' which, although constructed of posts, has the side walls of the mortuary chamber carried forward to form an ante-room—a style of architecture typical of the palaces of the Mycenaean culture in Greece—and which is also a model for Greek temples.

The burial mounds give an indication of the areas inhabited by the Mound People, whether or not they lived in their immediate vicinity. The large mounds lie everywhere in Denmark, along open hill ranges with wide views over sea and fjord, along navigable waterways, in the interior of the country and along ancient roads. Jutland's age-old main road, along the ridge of hills through the interior of the peninsula, is clearly marked by Bronze Age burial mounds and sites all the way from Ålborg southwards to the Danevirke at Slesvig: exactly the same route as was followed later by the Army Road and the Ox Road. Many rows of mounds in west Jutland point towards the coasts—to the embarkation ports in Thy and along the west coast. It was from here that trade and communications were maintained with the continent. Ports of call on the long sailing route were provided on the North Sea islands of Sild and Amrum where the Bronze Age is contemporary with that in Thy, and by the mouths of the rivers Elbe and Weser. From eastern Denmark and Skåne the main route was the one across the Baltic to Rügen and the river Oder, whence the rivers led on into Poland, Czechoslovakia, Austria and Hungary, with connections down to Greece and the Middle East.

49. The Ox Road west of Jelling

The striking positions of the burial mounds tell us of the power and the glory of the Mound People. The mounds were not simply last resting places; they were also monuments to a life lived in greatness. They were meant both to see and to be seen from far and wide. At that period the Danish countryside lay open as it did in the nineteenth century, before it was smothered under plantations of conifers. The Bronze Age landscape had a spacious park-like quality with scattered groups of trees and great expanses of pastureland where sheep and oxen grazed in great numbers. The moraine hills are not too large to be dominated by the burial mounds and given a special stature. In the positioning and design of the mounds the Bronze Age people showed a unique capacity for working hand in hand with nature. The mounds are not placed exactly on the highest point of a hill but a little to one side where the hill begins to slope, and that in itself gives them a distinctive appearance. This is further emphasized by the pointed summits which help produce a spherical profile in contrast to the rounded forms of the Ice Age hills.

That the Bronze Age mounds have preserved their original shape so well is because they were not made of heaped-up earth and gravel but carefully built of turfs, and also supported by stones placed in a ring or wall under the base. Originally, some of these stone circles were free-standing. In other mounds, the stone circle was replaced by a wattle fence made by driving in stakes and weaving twigs between them.

The enormous quantity of turf required for the building of the thousands of mounds must have laid waste vast grazing areas: it speaks of the sovereign mastery exerted by the Mound People over the land. One single mound required the turf from two and a half to four acres of good pasture land, which must have lain bare for a long time afterwards. The cutting of the thousands of turfs for each single mound would have involved enormous labour, so that there must have been a numerous subject class available for the work.

The nature of the Bronze Age landscape has been the subject of several investigations. One was a study of the sediment at the bottom of the Egtved girl's bucket and other

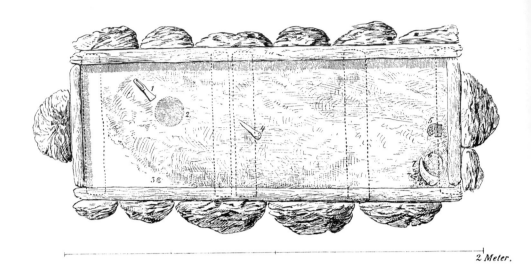

50. Plank coffin from Bredhøj

containers that consists exclusively of light-loving plants from commonland and the pollen of lime-tree blossom. Tests carried out on two south Jutland mounds reveal that they were erected on poor commonland covered with heath grass (*sieglingia decumbens*) and other poor grasses, heather, sedge, tormentil, dog violet, field woodrush or sweep's brush (*luzula campestris*) and a great deal of moss—a form of vegetation exclusively associated with hard grazing. Weeds were also numerous in the tests, and included sheep's sorrel (*rumex acetosella*), various kinds of willow herb and white goose-foot, showing that the ground had once been cultivated but had been allowed to grass over and become commonland. With intensive grazing, heather was widespread as well in the Mound People's time, as can be seen from the mounds built of heather-turf.

Old oak forests were another feature of the country. From these, timber was taken for the dwellings of the living and the dead. One such oak forest dating from the time of the Mound People was exposed at the bottom of the flat Lundegård Fen in Vendsyssel after it had been drained and its peat cut for fuel during the war. There stood the stumps of gigantic oaks among straight, fallen oak trunks. Alder and birch had grown there, too. It was apparent that the oak forest, which can be dated by carbon-14 analysis to the year 1290 B.C. plus or minus a hundred years, had decayed as a result of standing in stagnant water. This indicates that a brief rainy period corresponded with the epoch of the Mound People, although otherwise the warm climate of the Stone Age and the late Bronze Age was only seriously interrupted five hundred years later, near the beginning of the Iron Age.

The brief rainy period undoubtedly had a decisive effect both on the Mound People themselves and on our knowledge of them. Many things make it clear that they built up their distinguished and unique culture on a basis of cattle-breeding, and so the heavy rainfall—and not least in Jutland—substantially increased the grazing area for oxen and the quantity of fodder. At the same time, the rain contributed to the formation in large quantities of the hard-pan that enclosed the oak coffins, preserving them and the Mound People to the present day.

The Bronze Age was centuries emerging from the Stone Age. By the time of the Mound People it stood at the height of its glory. How great the step was from the one age to the next, and how great an organizational and commercial talent lay behind that step, is emphasized by the fact that whereas good flint had been for thousands of years the most important raw material in Denmark for tools and weapons, and could easily be obtained all over the country, every single ounce of metal had to be imported over long distances in exchange for home-produced goods. In the Stone Age, every tribe could obtain its material for weapons and tools; in the Bronze Age the sole group that could do so was the master class ruling over the country and controlling the import of bronze and gold. It is hard to understand how it was ever possible to obtain sufficient bronze—an alloy of about ninety per cent copper and ten per cent tin—to meet the colossal demand there must have been for metal. Not only was enough required to counteract the wastage of tools in constant use; it was also needed for new weapons and ornaments for each succeeding generation since so many personal belongings of bronze and gold accompanied their owners to the grave. Sacrifices to the powers watching over the life and fortunes of the Mound People swallowed up a large proportion of metal imports as well. These imports constantly increased through the late Bronze Age.

Finds from the Mound People's graves show how completely flint had been superseded. Only as a means of striking fire—flint against pyrites—did it still have value, and it is in these terms that most of the small flaked flints in the oak coffin burials must be interpreted. Other small flint blades were used by medicine men and doctors, as has already been said (see page 116). Possibly the use of flint tools was attributable primarily to the power that, it was believed, inhered in the stone. The same belief finds expression in a series of Bronze Age stone axes, usually of the rare material porphyry, which

51. Stone with rock-carving showing ship pictures from Truehøj Farm (approx. 1 : 2)

52. The narrow side of the Truehøj Farm stone with potent figure

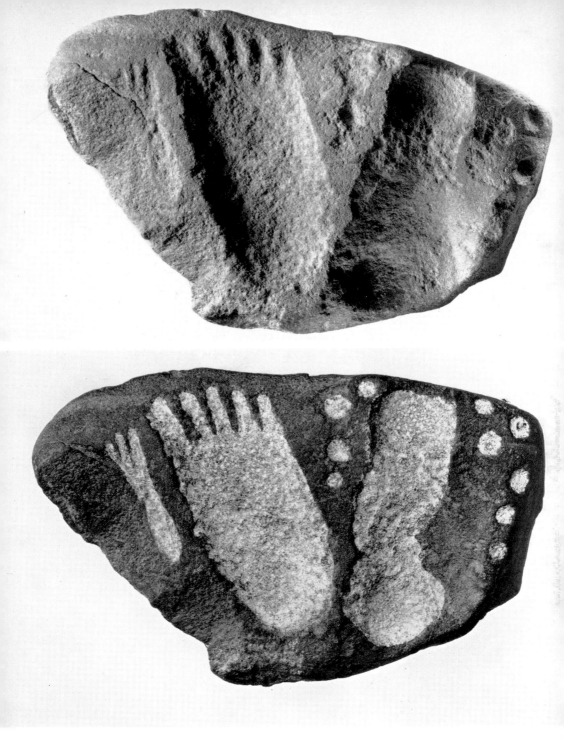

53. The other, broad side with foot-prints and cup marks
    (approx. 1 : 2)

in form are copies of bronze axes but are quite unsuitable for use as weapons or tools. Small flint tools for scraping skins and shaping pots have always been used, of course, but little more than they have been among the Jutland pottery women right up to now. For stronger tools, flint had been supplanted.

The foundations of the extensive Bronze Age trading were laid by the Battle-axe people and Bell Beaker people of the Stone Age who, as a result of their kinship with tribes in the metal-producing countries of Europe, were able to create the conditions necessary for leading the people of Scandinavia on to the distinctive and high-level Bronze Age culture. It is thus the popular migrations of the Stone Age that lie behind the emergence of the Bronze Age in northern Europe, where both the capacity and the talent existed to create an independent culture. The picture is everywhere the same: a rich trading class with military and maritime power that enabled it to secure the trade routes, and a large subservient class labouring at agriculture and cattle-breeding. The more prominent bronze-smiths, ship-builders and sailors would have formed the middle class. The society of the Mound People must have been very specialized.

But what riches could the Mound People offer the foreign traders in exchange for their gold and bronze—whether the actual exchange took place in Denmark or in foreign lands? The golden amber from the west coast of Jutland and elsewhere in Denmark has usually been regarded as the hard currency of the Mound People in this barter-trade. It has been pointed out that amber has been found in graves in many places in central and southern Europe as far south as Mycenae in Greece, while it is only very rarely found in the Scandinavian oak coffin graves. All that is known from them are a few buttons and beads and, even more rarely, thin inlays of amber in bronze articles. A find of six and a half pounds of amber in a clay vessel of the Bronze Age buried on the shore between Sæby and Frederikshavn is the sole large-scale discovery of its kind of this date and may be a treasure intended for the international barter market which for some reason was never sent. The rarity of amber in excavations of

54. The Herrestrup stone with rock-carvings of sun, horse, ship and cup (approx. 1 : 6)

the period in Denmark is interpreted as evidence that all that could be collected was sent south.

The fact is, however, that amber occurs in many other places on the coasts of Europe, such as for example East Prussia and the Channel coast of England, Sicily and the shores of the Black Sea. Since Sicilian amber is the only kind that can be positively identified, the rest of the amber in Central Europe may be from various sources. Probably a considerable proportion of it represents exports from Denmark in exchange for metal, particularly since the greater part of the Bronze Age gold finds come from Jutland, where amber is found in more profusion than anywhere else in the country.

Amber is 'fossilized' resin from the extensive coniferous forests that grew in the northern Baltic areas before the Ice Age, when avalanches carried it down to those areas in East Prussia and Denmark where it now occurs. Resin, too, must have been an important trading article in the Bronze Age. Round cakes of it the size of cow-pats, two to six of them in one place, have been found in a number of Danish fens. They are not, it seems, of Danish origin but most likely come from the forests of northern Scandinavia, so that they may be one of the raw materials that were imported from the north to be re-exported to the south. Similar cakes of resin are known from the Scandinavian peninsula, where, however, the dated finds belong to a later period.

It is hardly probable that amber alone was sufficient to maintain the trade first in finished goods manufactured throughout Europe and the eastern Mediterranean area, and subsequently in raw metal also. It has been suggested that Denmark traded in furs and the skins of rare animals as well, and train oil obtained by barter from the Scandinavian forest areas. This is possible, but it seems more likely that live animals were exported in great herds, as was the case later on, not least from Jutland, where finds and grave mounds indicate that the old Ox Road through central Jutland was finished in the period of the Mound People. That large horned animals played an important role for the master class of the Bronze Age is proved beyond doubt by finds from

55. The ox god, rock-carving on Löfåsen in Bohuslän

56. Rock-carving of man and cow at Hoghem in Bohuslän

the oak coffins, and the numerous representations of 'ox-men' in rock-carvings, as by horned helmets and the shape of *lurs*, too.

The importance of the ox in Scandinavian Bronze Age cults is exemplified by a rock-carving at Hoghem in Bohuslän which depicts on the same rock surface a spring wedding between a man and a woman, and a man mating with a cow. An account of such a scene between man and beast is to be found in the myths about the great Phoenician god Ba'al, the god of lightning, wind and rain, who 'roars in heaven' with the thunder and can also appear in the shape of a bull—as

57. Horned twin god from Grevensvænge (approx. 2:1)

related in the Old Testament. He represents the cosmic forces that create the life bursting forth in fields and pastures. In the myth, we hear about Ba'al's death, his sojourn in the kingdom of the dead, his resurrection and his ultimate ascent to the throne as ruler of gods and men. This cycle is described dramatically and represents the rhythm of life through the changing seasons.

During his sojourn in the land of the dead, Ba'al loved a heifer who bore him a son. He dressed the boy in his own garments so that he might occupy his place on the throne if he failed to return to the land of the living. The Ba'al myth was written down about 1,400 years before Christ and is thus a few centuries earlier than the period of the Mound People. The inscriptions preserving it were found on the Syrian coast of the Mediterranean, a little to the north of ancient Phoenicia, at Ras Shamrah, the site of the early town of Ugarit where large numbers of trading people and artisans from all over the eastern Mediterranean area used to gather. It was an international city state and its strange cult of ancient origin spread until faint ripples of it reached as far as Scandinavia. Something of this is reflected in the Hoghem picture and other Swedish rock-carvings in Bohuslän.

Perhaps the fact that the Mound People laid their dead, men and women alike, on freshly-flayed ox-hides in their oak coffins tells us more vividly than anything else what a central part these beasts played in their lives. The lovely hollowed-out wooden bowls decorated with tin pins would, it seems, have held fresh milk, and should be regarded as milk bowls. It is known among many cattle-breeding peoples that milk must not be put in clay or metal vessels. Horses and sheep must surely have followed in the train of oxen going south through Jutland, while dressed ox-hides and large quantities of wool probably also formed a salient part of the exports.

The possibility cannot be excluded that human beings—slender, fair young women and young boys of the lower labouring classes—were sent to the European slave markets in the same way. One or two early Bronze Age graves suggest that women from other countries may have been

58. Ship pictures, sun signs and cup marks on Madsebakke, Bornholm

brought to Denmark too. For example, amber beads of a distinctive type from a breast ornament of a kind worn by the women of southern Germany have been found in a mound at Andrup near Esbjerg, while a set of ornaments consisting of bronze plates and wheel pins found in another woman's grave at Smidstrup in south Zealand led Ebbe Lomborg to conclude 'that the Smidstrup grave contained a Lüneburg woman'. Foreign ornaments in other Bronze Age graves may also have belonged to women from distant lands, but whether these women were brought to Denmark by foreign traders from the European slave markets or were acquired abroad by the Mound People's own traders, we shall never know. Romantics will prefer to see love in a foreign market behind these women's graves.

The importance of the ship for Bronze Age overseas trade can scarcely be exaggerated. The ship was equally essential for keeping the many islands, peninsulas and mainlands of the Scandinavian Bronze Age area in contact with each other, and for the long-distance sea-going trade from Skåne and the Danish islands across the Baltic to Poland and the coasts and river mouths of Germany, and from north Jutland down along the west coast to north-west Germany; and across the North Sea to England, Scotland and Ireland. The multiplicity of imported finished goods in the graves bears testimony to these lengthy sea voyages, which required trained crews for navigation of the dangerous seas and coasts. The ship itself is represented on thousands of bronze articles, and is found carved on boulders and ice-scoured rock-faces—the Bronze Age rock-carvings.

The earliest known ship picture is engraved on a curved sword from Rørby in west Zealand. It shows a long rowing vessel with peaked prow and stern, the keel extended to form a battering ram at the prow, and with a rudder aft: a type of boat that is known in countless representations from the early Mediterranean but always appears without a sail in the north. The one on the Rørby sword seems to have had sixteen or seventeen pairs of oarsmen as well as a coxswain in the stern and a lookout man or skipper in the prow, all represented

59. Ship pictures, foot-prints and cup marks on Storløkkebakke,
Bornholm

simply by an oblique incision with a pin head. The crews of hundreds of Scandinavian ship pictures are represented in a like manner, sometimes only by a stroke, and sometimes with arms and oars as well as heads. Probably this type of boat reached the north by way of the rivers through eastern Europe, even if the exact route cannot be traced.

The reason the Bronze Age ship appears on so many bronze objects, almost exclusively razors in Denmark, and in rock-carvings is that it expresses a prayer to the powers on high to protect ships on their dangerous voyages by river and by sea. It was carried as a cult object in processions and offered to the gods as a sacrifice; but to give the sacred processions and sacrificial gifts enduring power they were also carved in stone. The more important anything was in daily life, the greater protective power it had, which is why the ship is to be seen carved in stone on graves—like for example the one on a small boulder from Truehøj Farm in Himmerland. However, the ship image has more than one meaning, as is the case with many other rock-carved representations. Ships may also be regarded, like the Truehøj vessels, as 'boats of Charon' for carrying the dead across the sea of death to another world. But in whatever way one interprets the thousands of ships dominating the image world of the Bronze Age, they tell us most of all about the class that controlled the metal trade and so ruled Scandinavia.

That agriculture played its part in the life of the Bronze Age people as well is indicated both by carvings and finds of ploughs and by traces of cultivated ground under the Mound People's graves. But it was the responsibility of a special class. Even at the beginning of the late Stone Age, five millennia ago, in the first Peasant Period, the earth was treated with a plough of the kind known as an ard that does not turn the soil over as the plough does but cuts broad furrows in it.

An ard of this kind of the first Bronze Age Period was found at Hvorslev in central Jutland, and is one of the types represented in Swedish Bronze Age rock-carvings. A carving on a small rock surface at Litsleby shows a hooked ard made of a forked stick, one branch of which is the share and the

60. Phallic man ploughing, Litsleby in Bohuslän

other the beam. The handle is at the rear end where it is held in one hand by a naked and highly phallic male figure, while in the other he has a branch or small tree. The plough is drawn by curved-horned oxen harnessed to a neck-yoke. The man is just starting the third furrow. It is obvious that he is engaged in the first ploughing of the year to awaken the earth's fruitfulness after the sleep of winter with the phallus of the plough, the ploughshare. Several details of the picture emphasize the importance of the fertility symbolism. The man's enormous phallus and the highly exaggerated reproductive organs of the oxen speak for themselves. The branch is a 'may tree', a feature of the spring fertility cult. A spring trickles down the side of the rock and adds to the scene the miraculous power of water. Water enhances fertility and in southern Germany until only a few hundred years ago a young man at the first ploughing of the year used to drive a team of young unmarried girls, who had been harnessed to an ard, through a stream when work was finished. The first three furrows were the most significant, and that is why this particular number is shown in the Litsleby carving.

Right up to 1911, it was the Emperor of China who ploughed the first three furrows of the sacred field the produce of which was to be used for sacrifices during the course of the year, while his magnificent ministers each ploughed three times three furrows. Similar customs are known from both Siam and India as well as from Homer's *Iliad*—which is mainly contemporary with the Bronze Age. On Bornholm the old folk used to say: 'Three furrows in Thor give a green spring', which expresses the hope that the old god of heaven will send the blessing of rain over the fields. The significance of the first ploughing is also shown by other pictures like, for example, the one from Tegneby in Bohuslän that depicts the sacred draught-animal of the sun, the stallion, drawing an ard tied to its tail.

Bronze Age grain production had its roots in Stone Age agriculture with its cultivation of single-grained wheat, emmer (*triticum dicoccum*), dwarf wheat, ordinary wheat, six-

61. Horse with sun wheel over ship picture, Kalleby in Bohuslän

62. A ship carried to sacrifice, Sotorp in Bohuslän

63. Stag hunt on stone from sacrificial pit at Bjergager Farm
(approx. 1:1)

rowed barley and millet. No doubt the descendants of the old Stone Age peasants continued to till the soil for the Mound People. In the Bronze Age, barley, both naked and awned, was the most important grain, though several of the old kinds were still cultivated, while oats, peas, beans and the oil plant, dodder, gradually appeared as new field crops.

In sea-girt Bronze Age Denmark, rich in fishing waters, fishing must naturally have continued to be practised as it had been in the time of the hunting and fishing peoples of the Stone Age. That the men of the Mound People were themselves interested in this ancient occupation, if only for sport, is proved by the bronze fish-hooks found in their graves. They hunted, too, but whenever hunting scenes are shown in Bronze Age stone carvings, it is not ordinary hunting that is represented but hunting events connected with the great seasonal festivals. There is a carving on a small stone from Bjergager Farm, west of Horsens in Jutland, of a huntsman with raised spear facing a stag and two hinds. Behind him is a representation of a snake and, in front of the stag, a tree. This carving dates from the latter part of the Bronze Age and is thus five hundred years after the period of the Mound People. The tree and the snake, which may be interpreted as the symbols of spring and of life, show that it is no ordinary hunt.

The stag as a sacrificial animal is known from finds in Denmark and from innumerable myths and representations throughout Europe. In Greece the stag, the noblest of animals, is depicted by the side of the lovely Artemis, the goddess of the wilds. In Denmark, stag hunting as a spring festival continued right up to the present time in the Vordingborg district where on Knudshoved Point a man was dressed up as a stag in a sheepskin coat with antlers on his head at Shrovetide and was chased from farm to farm while the other men shot at him with blank cartridges. In the end, he let himself be 'killed' and was carried on a sledge to the farm where the spring feast was being held. It is a good example of the preservation of an ancient custom.

7 · New Gods

THE cloth bundle containing the cremated bones of an eight-
or nine-year-old child, found at the foot of the oak coffin of
the young woman buried in Storhøj at Egtved, foreshadowed
the downfall of the Mound People. Only a couple of generations after her death all was changed: cremation had replaced
inhumation, the oak coffins had vanished and the grave had
become a clay urn containing the dead person's ashes. The
vigorous forms of weapons and ornaments became delicate
and refined; the continuous line of the spiral was ousted by
stars and circles. What it was that so suddenly altered the
Mound People's manners and customs, we can but guess. A
wave of change had swept from south-east Europe up into
the north, bringing with it other concepts of life and death.
New gods and goddesses came to rule over the fortunes of
the Mound People, even if the old ones were to continue to
hold sway for a while yet.

It was in fact a revolution that brought to an end the era
of the Mound People that had coincided with the second
great period of the Bronze Age. It was to be completed in the
third period, the last of the early Bronze Age, and was a
prelude to the late Bronze Age—a period by no means in-
ferior in greatness and glory to that of the Mound People,
although quite different from it. The revolution does not
appear in excavations as a sudden upheaval with abrupt
changes of style but is in many respects nearly imperceptible,
if unmistakable, which suggests that it was not violent. One

64. Snake goddess from Fårdal

65. Goddess from Kaiserberg in Holstein (approx. 3:1)

might be tempted to believe that a special group of the Mound People had suddenly seized power and asserted itself on returning from trading stations in foreign parts, though continuing to respect many earlier attitudes. The Bronze Age smiths went on practising their distinctive art while giving it a new content and style, as for example in the magnificent bronze *lurs*, unique in fullness of tone and in form. The agricultural workers and cattle breeders pursued their daily round unaffected. The fleet still brought goods to Denmark with its old crews and maintained exports as before.

We have already discussed the chieftain with the 'magician's bag' from Hvidegård. Although he was cremated, his grave was about six and a half feet long and so large enough to take an inhumation burial. Soon the graves were scaled down to suit the new custom of cremation.

A grave discovered towards the end of the last century in Trushøj at Skallerup in south Zealand was also large enough to contain an uncremated body. In it were found a bronze sword, a razor with a horse's-head handle, a pair of tweezers, a twisted gold arm ring and some woollen material, as well as a magnificent wheeled cauldron of bronze which had in it a man's burnt bones. This peculiar object, manufactured in south-east Europe in a technique the origin of which must be sought in the Mycenaean culture of Greece, consists of a hammered cauldron sailing forward on two ships with swan-figures in the bow and stern, the whole mounted on a wheel frame with two pairs of four-spoked wheels. As in the Trundholm sun-chariot, the wheels were added so that the sailing cauldron could be moved when it was used in the service of the cult. It was symbolic of the goddess of water and is seen depicted on countless central European bronze objects dating from the dry period that followed the rainy years of the Trundholm sun. We find the goddess herself later as the handle of a knife from Kaiserberg near Itzehoe in Holstein, a distinguished-looking, near-naked woman with enormous earrings, dressed only in a corded skirt like that of the Egtved girl and holding the vessel of sacred water before her in both hands.

66. Goddess from Horne in south Funen (approx. 8:1)

67. Backward-bending goddess from Grevensvænge (approx. 2:1)

68. Goddess enthroned from Fangel Torp (approx. 3:1)

Later on, in the late Bronze Age, female deities assumed a prominent place among the male gods until at last they actually came to dominate. This may be clearly seen in late Bronze Age representations from Denmark and is reflected in the sacrificial objects placed beside sacred springs and elsewhere in earth and fen. For whereas the objects sacrificed at the beginning of the Bronze Age consisted exclusively of weapons and other gifts to male divinities, women's ornaments and associated items gradually replaced them almost entirely in the sacrificial groves of the late Bronze Age.

A site at Maglehøj in the west part of north Zealand, excavated by Vilhelm Boye in 1888, shows that women also took over the role of medicine man. At the bottom of the mound stood a small stone coffin covered with a heavy block of stone, eel-grass and a heap of stones that had protected the grave from earth sifting down. Inside was a woman's belt box, a double-headed fastener, a knife and a fibula of bronze on top of the cremated bones, which had been wrapped in a piece of woollen clothing. Within the bronze box—of a kind that women carried on their backs—were the sorcerer's charms: two horse's teeth, some weasel (marten) bones, the claw-joint of a member of the cat family (possibly a lynx), bones from a young mammal (a lamb or deer?), a piece less than half an inch long of a bird's windpipe, some vertebrae from a snake, two burnt fragments of bone (human?), a twig of mountain ash, charred aspen, two pebbles of quartz, a lump of clay, two pieces of pyrites, a sheet of bronze and a piece of bronze wire bent at one end to form a small hook. Both the belt-fastener and the bronze box were ornamented with star patterns.

The fact that cremation had become universal reveals that a new faith in life after death had spread throughout the land. The dead no longer had their dwelling-place in the burial mounds, but instead the soul was freed from the body with the help of fire so that it could fly unhampered to the kingdom of the dead and be born again into the world where the invisible powers held sway. We find such an explanation given in the funeral hymns of the Hindus, which

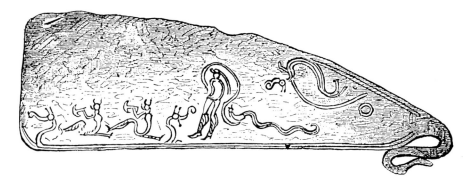

69. Pictorial representation on razor from Vestrup (approx. 2:1)

tell us that fire, as the servant of God, conveys the dead to the kingdom where gods and ancestors dwell. The same belief occurs amongst the Indian tribes of the Pacific coast of America, who also practise cremation:

'Unless the body is burnt the soul will never reach the land of the dead' . . . 'In the hot smoke it rises up to the shining sun to rejoice in its warmth and light; then it flies away to the happy land in the west'.

A find in a cremation grave in Himmerland suggests that the survivors, in their concern for the dead, sought to assist this celestial flight. Mixed with the burnt bones of a young person were those of the wings of at least six jackdaws and two crows, as well as two crows' feet. We cannot doubt the intention behind the laying of so many wings on the pyre: the twelve small wings and four large ones were to bear his soul safely to the land of the dead.

How extensive the Bronze Age Parnassus gradually became —with a goddess as its central feature—is brought out by two finds of small bronze figures. The first was made on a steep slope above the Nørreår valley at Fårdal between Viborg and Randers. It consisted of women's ornaments, a small kneeling goddess with large, shining eyes overlaid with gold dressed only in a corded skirt, and also a snake and three animal heads. Probably the woman and the animal figures formed

163

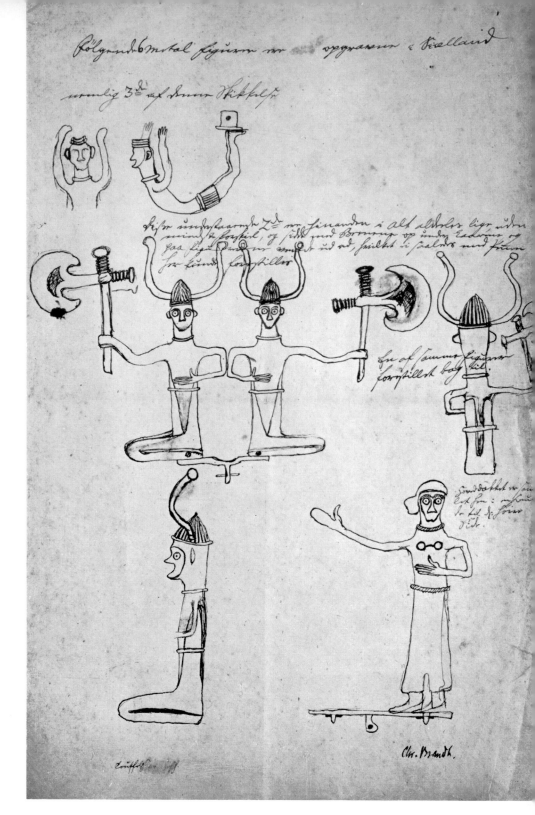

70. Sketches of gods from Grevensvænge

part of a group, which it is possible to reconstruct on the basis of contemporary rock-carvings. The figures must have been attached to the same cult boat, the woman and the snake in the middle and the animal heads in the prow and stern. This marks the entry into the north of the Oriental goddess of fecundity with the snake.

The other find was made at Grevensvænge in south Zealand, but this has been almost totally lost. Fortunately, we have drawings of the figures that were made at the end of the eighteenth century. It consisted of three women in corded skirts bending backwards, two men in helmets carrying axes and linked together like a pair of twins, and a standing female figure mounted on a small bronze plate that shows there was originally another figure by her side, probably a snake. All that remains of this unique find of beautifully modelled bronze figures is one of the backward-bending female figures and one helmeted man without his axe. These figures too formed part of a cult boat with the women in corded skirts at the prow and stern, the axe-carrying twin gods representing the heavenly powers on the foremost thwart, and the goddess with the snake behind them. There is a similar composition on a razor found at Vestrup in Himmerland. In this the principal motif is the two-horned, axe-bearing twin gods in a boat. To their rear stands the goddess holding a great snake. The sun and its draught animal, the horse, are also included, though not in a very prominent position, being contracted nearly beyond recognition to fit into the small triangle under the swan-shaped handle.

The engraving on the Vestrup razor and the Grevensvænge figures show that Bronze Age people worshipped both the heavenly powers and the great earth goddess. The sun with the horse and the axe-bearing twin gods come from the East, from the endless steppes of Asia, while the origins of the snake-goddess must be sought in central Asia, where as mother-goddess she occupied a dominating position in many of the earliest cultures under a multiplicity of names. One of her closest relatives is the snake- and earth-goddess of the Cretan Bronze Age. In the ancient town of Knossos, the

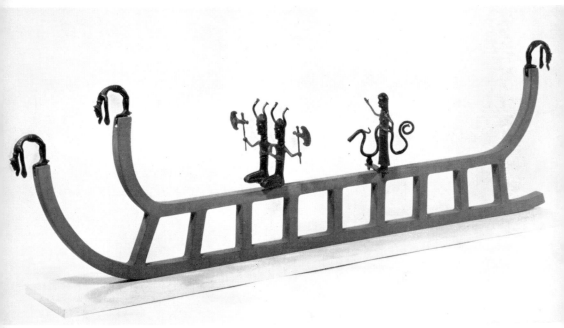

71. Reconstructed cult boats from Fårdal and Grevensvænge

capital of King Minos according to legend, she is represented
in faience wearing a skirt to the ground, her breasts bared and
holding a snake in her outstretched hands. She is also
represented in a boat executed in bronze, as in Scandinavia.

As early as the Stone Age the earth goddess found her way
to Denmark both overland from southern Europe with the
early farming cultures, and by sea from western Europe,
where her trail may be followed along the Mediterranean
coasts. That she still held power in the days of the Mound
People is indicated by carvings on stones from their graves.
Her simplest sign is the cup mark, a round hollow the size of
a five kroner piece (about two inches across), cut into stone—
often a number of them together. One such cup mark was
carved over a grave at Debel on Fuur in Limfjord. On this is
also depicted the sacred spring wedding, the union of man
and woman, in a severely simplified and almost unrecog-
nizable form together with the cross sign, the symbol of life.
The spring wedding is presented unequivocally on a small,
round slab of stone from Maltegård in north Zealand, on
which are shown a man and a woman, both with their
sexual characteristics strongly emphasized, stretching out
their arms to each other, the scene surrounded by a wreath of
spring flowers. Behind the woman stands a 'may tree'.
Swedish rock-carvings depict the sacred wedding, representing the origin of life, as it was celebrated year after year by
the participants at the great spring festival held to reawaken
the life-giving forces of nature.

The world of the gods in the Scandinavian Bronze Age is of
very varied origins. Representatives of the heavenly gods of
the cattle breeders inhabit it together with the earth goddess
of agriculture. Many of the carvings illustrate this merging of
the two religions, like for example a rock-carving at Slänge in
Bohuslän that obviously represents the meeting of the goddess
of earth and the god of heaven. Here the god of heaven bears
the sign of the wheel and the goddess has long hair.

Yet another goddess from the last period of the Bronze Age
must be mentioned who was found at the first ploughing of
the edge of an extensive patch of bog at Fangel on Funen,

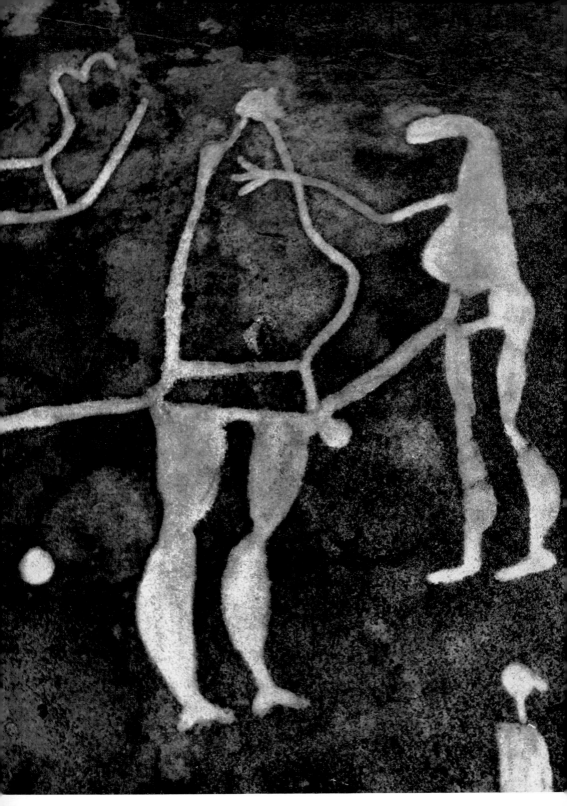

72. The sacred spring wedding on a rock-carving at Hvarlös in Bohuslän

73. And on a grave slab from Debel on Fuur

74. The goddess of earth meets the god of heaven, Slänge
in Bohuslän

75. Horned men blowing *lurs*, and ship, Kalleby in Bohuslän

together with a large number of women's ornaments, neck and wrist rings and a corn sickle—which suggest that as goddess of fertility she also reigned over agriculture and was the mother of the corn. The goddess from Fangel is naked, wearing only a neck ring and earrings, and sits enthroned with her hands over her life-giving breasts.

In the succeeding period, the Iron Age, this goddess— Mother Earth—became all-powerful. It was to her that the Bog People were sacrificed, a fate that was to preserve them to the present day. But she, too, was responsible for shattering the glorious rule of the Mound People and their descendants. Bronze was to be replaced by iron as the most important material for weapons and tools. Since iron could be extracted from bog ore all over the country, the ancient peasant communities became independent of the trading people, as we have seen. The peculiar culture of the Bronze Age perished: rocks were carved no more, and images and signs on bronze objects degenerated into mere ornament, finally disappearing altogether. The *lurs*, those magnificent musical instruments that had for generations summoned the Bronze Age people to the great annual festivals and other ceremonies, were consigned at the religious change-over to the bogs as sacrifices to the gods who had given the Mound People their power and their glory.

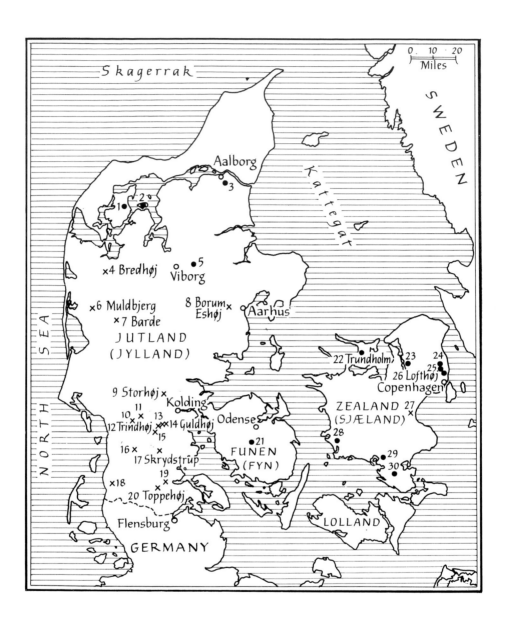

Map of Denmark showing the sites referred to in the text (*See* pp. 175–6)

List of Finds

SIGNS and abbreviations below and opposite: X = oak coffins,
● = other finds, *f.* = year of find, *p.* = parish, *h.* = hundred.

1. TØDSØ: *f.* 1950, *p.* Tødsø, *h.* Mors Nørre.
2. DEBEL: *f.* 1930, *p.* Fuur, *h.* Harre.
3. SOLHØJ: *f.* 1899, *p.* Sønder Tranders, *h.* Fleskum.
4. BREDHØJ: *f.* 1885, *p.* Måbjerg, *h.* Hjerm.
5. FÅRDAL: *f.* 1926, *p.* Viskum, *h.* Sønderlyng.
6. MULDBJERG: *f.* 1883, *p.* Hover, *h.* Hind.
7. BARDE STORE HØJ: *f.* 1882, *p.* Vorgod, *h.* Hammerum.
8. BORUM ESHØJ: *f.* 1871, *p.* Borum, *h.* Framlev.
9. STORHØJ: *f.* 1921, *p.* Egtved, *h.* Jerlev.
10. FLADSHØJ: *f.* 1860, *p.* Føvling, *h.* Malt.
11. FOLDINGBRO KROGÅRD: *f.* 1823, *p.* Folding, *h.* Malt.
12. TRINDHØJ: *f.* 1861, *p.* Vamdrup, *h.* Anst.
13. STORE KONGEHØJ: *f.* 1861, *p.* Vamdrup, *h.* Anst.
14. GULDHØJ: *f.* 1891, *p.* Vamdrup, *h.* Anst.
15. JELS: *f.* 1934, *p.* Jels, *h.* Gram.
16. LILLE DRAGSHØJ: *f.* 1860, *p.* Højrup, *h.* Hvidding.
17. SKRYDSTRUP: *f.* 1935, *p.* Skrydstrup, *h.* Gram.
18. NØRAGERHØJ: *f.* 1856, *p.* Emmerlev, *h.* Højer.
19. STAMPLUND: *f.* 1837, *p.* Hjortkær, *h.* Rise.
20. TOPPEHØJ: *f.* 1827, *p.* Bjolderup, *h.* Rise.
21. FANGEL TORP: *f.* 1913, *p.* Fangel, *h.* Odense.
22. TRUNDHOLM: *f.* 1902, *p.* Højby, *h.* Ods.
23. MAGLEHØJ: *f.* 1888, *p.* Oppesundby, *h.* Lynge-Frederiksborg.

24. JÆGERSBORG HEGN: *f.* 1863, *p.* Søllerød, *h.* Sokkelund.
25. HVIDEGÅRD: *f.* 1845, *p.* Lyngby, *h.* Sokkelund.
26. LØFTHØJ: *f.* 1886, *p.* Gentofte, *h.* Sokkelund.
27. ØLBY: *f.* 1880, *p.* Højelse, *h.* Ramsø.
28. BORGBJERG: *f.* 1842, *p.* Boeslunde, *h.* Slagelse.
29. GREVENSVÆNGE: *f.* 1770s, *p.* Rønnebak, *h.* Hammer.
30. TRUSHØJ: *f.* 1895, *p.* Skallerup, Udby, *h.* Baarse.

Bibliography

Abbreviation:
Årb. = *Aarbøger for nordisk Oldkyndighed og Historie,*
Copenhagen

1. Bertil Almgren, 'Hällristningar och bronsåldersdräkt'
   (Rock carvings and Bronze Age costume), *TOR*, vol. 6,
   1960
2. Christian Blinkenberg, 'En etruskisk Kjedelvogn' (An
   Etruscan wheeled cauldron), *Årb.*, 1895
3. Vilhelm Boye, 'Maglehøj-Fundet' (The Maglehøj find),
   Årb., 1889
4. Vilhelm Boye, *Fund af Egekister fra Bronzealderen i Danmark*
   (Finds of [Bronze Age] oak coffins in Denmark),
   Copenhagen, 1896
5. H. C. Broholm and Margrethe Hald, *Danske Bronzealders
   Dragter* (Danish Bronze Age costumes), Copenhagen,
   1935
6. H. C. Broholm and Margrethe Hald, *Skrydstrupfundet*
   (The Skrydstrup find), Copenhagen, 1939
7. H. C. Broholm, *Danmarks Bronzealder* (The Bronze Age
   in Denmark), vols. 1–4, Copenhagen, 1943–49
8. Johannes Brøndsted, *Danmarks Oldtid*, vol. 2, *Bronzealderen*
   (Early Denmark, vol. 2, the Bronze Age), Copenhagen,
   1958
9. Kurt Bröste, *Prehistoric Man in Denmark*, Copenhagen,
   1956

10. H. Duncan, *Beretning om et i en hedensk Gravhøj paa Lundtofte Mark nylig fundet Skelet* (Account of a skeleton found recently in a heathen burial mound on Lundtofte farm), Copenhagen, 1840

11. Gutorm Gjessing, 'Hesten i forhistorisk kunst og kultus' (The horse in prehistoric art and cult), *Viking*, vol. 7, 1943

12. P. V. Glob, *Ard og Plov i Nordens Oldtid* (Ard and plough in early Scandinavia), Århus, 1951

13. P. V. Glob, *Helleristninger i Danmark* (Rock-carvings in Denmark), Århus, 1969

14. Søren Hansen, 'Om forhistorisk Trepanation i Danmark' (On prehistoric trepanning in Denmark), *Årb.*, 1889

15. C. F. Herbst, 'Hvidegårdsfundet' (The Hvidegård find), *Annaler*, 1848

16. Jørgen Jensen, 'Bronze for Rav' (Bronze for amber), *Skalk*, 1967

17. Karl Kersten, *Zur älteren nordischen Bronzezeit* (On the early Scandinavian Bronze Age), Neumünster, 1936

18. Ebbe Lomborg, 'Troldmandstasken' (The magician's bag), *Skalk*, 1966, no. 5

19. Ebbe Lomborg, 'Ravfund ved Vestkysten' (Amber finds on the west coast), *Skalk*, 1967

20. Ebbe Lomborg, 'Den tidlige bronzealders kronologi' (Chronology of the Early Bronze Age), *Årb.*, 1968

21. C.-A. Moberg, *Kivikgraven, Svenska fornminnesplatser nr. 1* (The Kivik grave, sites of early monuments in Sweden, no. 1), 1963

22. Sophus Müller, *Solbilledet fra Trundholm* (The sun image from Trundholm), Copenhagen, 1903

23. C. J. Thomsen, *Ledetraad til Nordisk Oldkyndighed* (Guide lines to knowledge of Scandinavian antiquities), Copenhagen, 1836

24. Thomas Thomsen, *Egekistefundet fra Egtved, fra den ældre Bronzealder* (The oak coffin find from Egtved, from the Early Bronze Age), Copenhagen, 1929

Index

179